# history at source

Hodder & Stoughton
A MEMBER OF THE HODDER HEADLINE GROUP

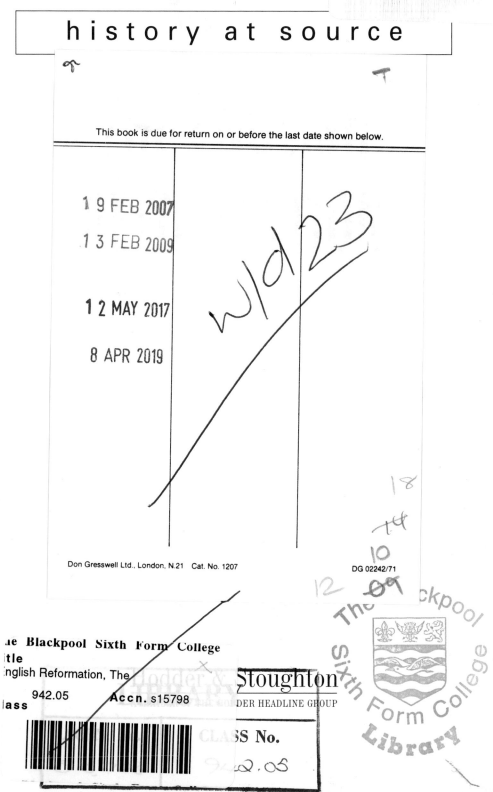

# ACKNOWLEDGEMENTS

The cover illustration is a portrait of William Wareham by courtesy of the National Portrait Gallery, London.

The publishers wish to thank the following for permission reproduce the following copyright illustrations in this volume:
British Library p.44, 81, 82b, 103, 109; Cambridge University Library p.6, p.105; E.T. Archive p.78; Folger Shakespeare Library, Washington p.17. Hunting Aerofilms p.4t; National Portrait Gallery p.56, 57; Royal Collection Enterprises p.82; Victoria & Albert Museum p.98; Nicholas Ervian, courtesy Woodmansterne Ltd p.8.

The publishers would like to thank the following for permission to reproduce material in this volume:
Barrie and Jenkins for an extract from D Wilson *The People and the Book* (1976); Batsford Ltd for an extract from AG Dickens *The English Reformation* (1989); Blackwell Publishers for extracts from CRN Routh (ed.) *They Saw It Happen*, Vol. II (1956) and D Loades *Mary Tudor: A Life* (1989); Cambridge University Press for extracts from GR Elton *The Tudor Constitution* (2nd edition, 1982); Macmillan Press Ltd for an extract from D Cook (ed.) *Documents and Debates. Sixteenth Century England 1450-1600* (1980) and C Derlin The Life of Robert Southwell (1967); Methuen London, reprinted by permission of Reed Consumer Books for an extract from WC Sellar and RJ Yeatman *1066 and All That* (1930); extracts from Christopher Haigh *English Reformations* (1993) by permission of Oxford University Press; Rogers, Coleridge and White for an extract translated by Philip Caraman from John Gerard *The Autobiography of an Elizabethan* (Longman 1951); Routledge for extracts from CH Williams (ed.) *English Historical Documents*, Vol. 5 1485-1558 (1967); Yale University Press for an extract from E Duffy *The Stripping of the Alters* (1992).

Every effort has been made to trace and acknowledge ownership of copyright. The publishers will be glad to make suitable arrangements with any copyright holders whom it has not been possible to contact.

**British Library Cataloguing in Publication Data**
A catalogue for this title is available from the British Library

ISBN 0 340 63082 5

First published 1997

Impression number   10   9   8   7   6   5   4   3   2   1
Year                         2002   2001   2000   1999   1998   1997

Typeset by Wearset, Boldon, Tyne and Wear.
Printed in Great Britain for Hodder & Stoughton Educational, a division of Hodder Headline Plc, 338 Euston Road, London NW1 3BH by Redwood Books, Trowbridge, Wiltshire.

# CONTENTS

# APPROACHING SOURCE-BASED

## QUESTIONS

Sources are now an integral part of most History examination courses and students will normally have been introduced to them before starting such courses. By the time of the examination students should be familiar with a wide variety of types of source and have had practice in evaluating and commenting on them. However, students still complain about their inability to deal with sources and seem to forget some of the basic rules for doing so. The following points are worth remembering, whether using sources as part of a course or in an examination.

Read the content of the source carefully as needless mistakes can result from careless reading. Ignoring a word or a phrase can change the meaning of a source. If a source is reporting a conversation be certain who is saying what. The style in a source can be important. Should the words be taken as written or is there any humour or irony intended?

Every source, whatever kind it is, has been produced in a particular context for a particular purpose. Find out as much as possible about context and purpose before commenting. Who produced it? Whom did they want to read/see/hear the source? Was it meant to be a permanent record? Was it mainly reacting to something or initiating something?

Read the question carefully. If the question is about more than one source then be sure to refer to all the sources mentioned as failure to do so will lose marks in an examination. Some questions require an answer based on the sources alone, e.g. 'What do these sources tell us about . . . ?' Others will require candidates to set them in context and comment on the sources in the light of their own knowledge, e.g. 'How adequately do these sources explain . . . ?'

Evaluation is important. This requires commenting on the sources not just paraphrasing them. Is the question simply about the content or does it call for comment on the context as well? Some questions are explicit about the kind of evaluation called for and ask how useful a source is, or about its bias or its reliability. Responding with the appropriate evaluation may mean covering more than one aspect. Reliability and utility overlap for example, and the usefulness of a source may depend to some extent on its reliability. Remember, too, that a biased source can be reliable – as long as the bias is self-evident.

Take note of the marks allocated for each question as these will give some indication of how long answers should be, although marks may also take into account the relative difficulty of a question.

Be prepared to use pictures and other non-written sources. They were and are important and can justify close analysis.

Source-based exercises are not just an end in themselves. Sources should also contribute to a candidate's general historical understanding and provide material for essays and discussion. A number of examination boards do mention that appropriate reference to original sources is something they look for in essay answers.

# INTRODUCTION

The Tudor period is one of the most popular studied at A-level and the religious changes are a key feature of that period. However, many students find these changes difficult to understand. The issues at stake and the apparent bigotry of many of the individuals concerned can be hard to comprehend in a modern, pluralist society. But the effort needs to be made and this book is an attempt to help that understanding. The nature of the subject means that a certain amount of specialist vocabulary is needed fully to understand some of these sources and to answer some of the questions and so this book should be used alongside a reliable textbook.

At least one chapter has been included for each of the main stages of the Reformation, starting with an introduction on the pre-Reformation Church. The reigns of Henry VIII and Elizabeth I may seem to be over-represented but the number of chapters and topics covered are justified by the weighting given to them in A-level syllabuses and examinations. Cranmer has a chapter to himself [Chapter 7] as an example of the contribution an individual can make to a major historical event. The themes of the chapters on the Royal Supremacy [Chapter 10] and the English Bible [Chapter 13] are important in themselves as well as providing a way of looking at the development of ideas during the whole of the Reformation period.

The documents chosen reflect as wide a variety as possible. Some of them will already be familiar to teachers if not to students, but there are others that are not so often found in collections of this kind. The purpose is not only to provide practice at working on different types of sources but also to introduce students to the wide range available.

Most students by this stage are familiar with the concept that the same events can be interpreted in many different ways. This is the theme of the historiography chapter dealing with interpretations of the reign of Mary I [Chapter 14]; the other chapters should also provide enough material to reflect a diversity of approaches.

The overall purpose of this collection is to provide the student with examples of the kinds of sources that might appear in an examination paper and the questions at the end of each chapter have been drawn up with the same aim in mind. However, the collection is not a set course and should be adapted to the needs of the student – documents left out, new combinations of documents made, different questions asked or mark allocations altered – as appropriate.

# *Chronology of the English Reformation*

| | | |
|---|---|---|
| 1521 | July | Henry VIII published The Defence of the Seven Sacraments against Luther |
| | Oct. | The Pope gave Henry the title Defender of the Faith |
| 1529 | May | Cardinal Campeggio presided over a court to decide on the validity of Henry's marriage to Catherine of Aragon |
| | July | The Court was adjourned to Rome |
| | Nov. | The opening of the Reformation Parliament |
| 1532 | May | First Act in Restraint of Annates |
| 1533 | Jan. | Henry VIII married Anne Boleyn |
| | March | Cranmer consecrated Archbishop of Canterbury |
| | | Act in Restraint of Appeals |
| 1534 | March | Second Act in Restraint of Annates |
| | Nov. | Act of Supremacy |
| | | Treason Act |
| 1535 | Jan. | Thomas Cromwell appointed Vice-gerent in Spirituals |
| | May | Visitation of religious houses began |
| | June | Execution of John Fisher |
| | July | Execution of Thomas More |
| 1536 | March | Act for the Dissolution of the Lesser Monasteries |
| | May | Execution of Anne Boleyn |
| | July | Ten Articles |
| | Aug. | First Injunctions to the Clergy |
| | Oct.–Dec. | Pilgrimage of Grace |
| 1537 | Sep. | Bishops' Book |
| 1538 | Sep. | Second Injunctions to the Clergy |
| 1539 | April | The Great Bible |
| | June | Act of Six Articles |
| 1540 | March | Surrender of the last religious house – Waltham Abbey |
| 1543 | May | The King's Book |
| 1547 | Jan. | Death of Henry VIII. Accession of Edward VI |
| | Dec. | Act for the Dissolution of the Chantries |
| 1549 | Jan. | First Prayer Book |
| | June–Aug. | Western Rebellion |
| 1552 | Nov. | Second Prayer Book |
| 1553 | July | Death of Edward VI. Accession of Mary I |
| | Oct. | Repeal of Edwardian religious legislation |
| 1554 | Jan. | Wyatt's rebellion |
| | Nov. | England's official restoration to the Catholic Church |
| 1555 | Feb. | Beginning of the Marian persecutions |
| | Dec. | Cranmer deprived of archbishopric |
| | | Pole appointed Archbishop of Canterbury |

| | | |
|---|---|---|
| *1556* | *March* | Execution of Cranmer |
| *1558* | *Nov.* | Death of Mary I. Accession of Elizabeth I |
| | | Death of Cardinal Pole |
| *1559* | *April* | Act of Supremacy |
| | | Act of Uniformity |
| *1563* | *Feb.* | Thirty-Nine Articles |
| | | Foxe's Acts and Monuments |
| *1566* | *March* | Archbishop Parker's Book of Advertisements |
| *1568* | *May* | Mary, Queen of Scots, arrived in England |
| | *Sep.* | William Allen founded seminary for English priests at Douai |
| *1569* | *Oct.–Dec.* | Rising of the Northern Earls |
| *1570* | *Feb.* | Papal Bull of Excommunication |
| *1572* | *June* | Puritan Admonition to Parliament |
| *1574* | | Arrival of first missionary priests from Douai |
| *1575* | *Dec.* | Grindal appointed Archbishop of Canterbury |
| *1576* | *Dec.* | Grindal refused to take action against prophesyings |
| *1577* | *June* | Grindal suspended |
| *1580* | *June* | Arrival of the first Jesuit missionaries |
| *1583* | *Aug.* | John Whitgift appointed Archbishop of Canterbury |
| | | Whitgift's Articles |
| *1587* | *Nov.* | Execution of Mary, Queen of Scots |
| *1588* | *Oct.* | First of the Martin Marprelate tracts |
| | *May–Sep.* | Spanish Armada |
| *1595* | *Nov.* | Lambeth Articles |
| *1603* | *March* | Death of Elizabeth I |

# 1 RELIGION IN PRE-REFORMATION
# ENGLAND

In the sixteenth century England experienced a reformation in religion
– a Catholic country, apparently loyal to the Pope, became a Protestant
nation that accepted the monarch as the Supreme Governor of the
Church. Did this mean that the Church had needed reform, or that the
people of England had wanted reform? At one time perhaps the answer
would have been yes, on both counts. The mere fact of a successful
reformation was taken to show both that Protestantism had won a well-
deserved victory and therefore the Catholic Church had been corrupt
[E], and also that the people had happily embraced the reformed
Church and must therefore have been dissatisfied with the old pre-
Reformation Church.

Most historians are now prepared to be rather more generous to the
Church of the early sixteenth century. Instead of being portrayed as a
lifeless institution of little real relevance to the people, it is seen as
answering more than adequately the religious needs of the vast majority
of its members. Parish life in particular was flourishing. The services and
processions that marked the annual cycle of feasts were well supported
by the parishioners who contributed to their upkeep and to the
maintenance and decoration of the churches where they took place [A,
I-L]. The clergy [C-D, F-G], even if few were educated as far as a
university degree, were nevertheless largely competent and related more
effectively to their parishioners than might a learned but socially more
isolated pastor.

This view does not deny that there was demand for reform in some
circles. Loyal Catholics were capable of pointing to their Church's
shortcomings and demanding in no uncertain terms that it should live
up to its own ideals. Other demands went further. Attacks on the failures
of some institutions became attacks on the very existence of the
institutions [B]; criticisms of the excesses associated with certain beliefs
became attacks on the beliefs themselves [H]. These critics wanted
radical changes both in organisation and in doctrine.

Where, in all this, do we put the emphasis? Granted that the evidence
is there to support a number of different views, how do we decide which
view, or combination of views, best represents the pre-Reformation
Church? There is no lack of contemporary or near-contemporary
criticism of the Church, but is it not the nature of criticism to stand out,
to be noticed and recorded? How can we judge satisfaction with a

situation? Is that as likely to find explicit expression as dissatisfaction, or do we have to build up a picture from a host of small details? What is the borderline between satisfaction and unthinking conformity?

Some judgement on this matter of defining the pre-Reformation Church is necessary since it has implications for how and why the Reformation happened. Was it a process that forced people to abandon cherished beliefs and traditions or did it provide the opportunity for which these people were already looking? Did the architects of the Reformation simply lead or did they have to push?

## A The English and their religion

Although they all attend Mass every day, and say many Paternosters in public (the women carrying long rosaries in their hands, and any who can read taking the office of Our Lady with them, and with some companion reciting it in the church verse by verse, in a low voice, after the manner of churchmen), they always hear mass on Sunday in their parish church, and give liberal alms . . . nor do they omit any form incumbent upon good Christians; there are however many who have various opinions concerning religion.

. . . above all are their riches displayed in the church treasures; for there is not a parish church in the kingdom so mean as not to possess crucifixes, candlesticks, censers, patens, and cups of silver; nor is there a convent of mendicant friars so poor, as not to have all these same articles in silver, besides many other ornaments worthy of a cathedral church in the same metal. Your Magnificence may therefore imagine what the decorations of those enormously rich Benedictine, Carthusian and Cistercian monasteries must be. These are indeed more like baronial palaces than religious houses, as your Magnificence may have perceived at that of St Thomas of Canterbury. And I have been informed that amongst other things, many of these monasteries possess unicorn's horns, of an extraordinary size. I have also been told that they have some splendid tombs of English saints, such as St Oswald, St Edmund, and St Edward, all kings and martyrs.

I saw one day . . . at Westminster, a place out of London, the tomb of Saint King Edward the Confessor, in the church of the aforesaid place Westminster; and indeed, neither St Martin of Tours, a church in France, which I have heard is one of the richest in existence, nor anything else that I have ever seen, can be put into any sort of comparison with it. But the magnificence of the tomb of St Thomas the Martyr, Archbishop of Canterbury, is that which surpasses all belief. This, notwithstanding its great size is entirely covered over with plates of pure gold; but the gold is scarcely visible from the variety of precious stones with which it is studded, such as sapphires, diamonds, rubies, balas-rubies and emeralds; and on every side that the eye turns, something more beautiful than the other appears.

From a description of England, probably sent to the Venetian Senate by Andrea Trevisano, *c.*1500

## B   Attacks on the Church

As for preaching [bishops] take no care,
They would see a course at an hare
　　Rather than to make a sermon . . .

They drink in gay golden bowls
The blood of poor simple souls,
　　Perishing for lack of sustenance.
Their hungry cures they never teach
Nor will suffer none other to preach
　　But such as can lie and flatter . . .

As for religious folk, to be brief,
In all England they have the chief
　　And most pleasant commodities,
The goodly soils, the goodly lands
Wrongfully they hold in their hands . . .

They are the cause of misery
Of whoredom, theft and beggary
　　To the common weal's hindrance.
No fruitful work they use,
All honest labour they refuse,
　　Given wholly to sluggishness.
They are neither ghostly nor divine
But like to brute beasts and swine
　　Weltering in sinful wretchedness . . .

Friars? Now they are the worst of all,
Ruffian wretches and rascal
　　Lodesmen of all knavishness.
Though they be no possessioners
Yet are they intolerable beggars,
　　Living on rapine and deceit,
Worshipful matrons to beguile,
Honourable virgins to defile.

From William Roy and Jerome Barlow: *Rede me and be not wrothe* (Strasbourg, 1528)

## C  Reformation from the inside

Ye are come together today, fathers and right wise men, to enter council; in the which, what you will do and what matters you will handle, yet we understand not. But we wish that once, remembering your name and profession, you would mind the reformation of the Church's matter. For it was never more need, and the state of the Church did never desire more your endeavours. For the Spouse of Christ, the Church, whom you would should be *without spot or wrinkle*, is made foul and evil-favoured . . .

Priests and bishops are the light of the world . . . if priests and bishops, that should be as lights, run in the dark way of the world, how dark then shall the secular people be? . . .

O covetousness! St Paul justly called thee the root of all evil. Of thee cometh this heaping of benefices upon benefices. . . . Of thee all the sueing for tithes, for offering, for mortuaries, for dilapidations, by the right and title of the Church. . . . Of thee cometh the corruptness of courts, and these daily new inventions wherewith the simple people are so sore vexed . . .

We are also nowadays grieved of heretics, men mad with marvellous foolishness. But the heresies of them are not so pestilent and pernicious unto us and the people as the evil and wicked life of priests. . . . St Bernard . . . sheweth plainly to be two manner of heresies; the one to be of perverse teaching, and the other of naughty life: of which this latter is worse and more perilous. The which reigneth now in the Church in priests not living priestly but secularly, to the utter and miserable destruction of the Church.

The way whereby the Church may be reformed into better fashion is not for to make new laws. For there be laws many enough and out of number. . . . For the evils that are now in the Church were before in time past; and there is no fault but that fathers have provided very good remedies for it . . .

Let the laws be rehearsed, that command that benefices of the Church be given to those that are worthy; and that promotions be made in the Church by the right balance of virtue, not by carnal affection . . .

Let the laws be rehearsed, that warreth against the spot of Simony . . .

Let the laws be rehearsed that command personal residence of curates in their churches . . .

Let be rehearsed the laws and holy rules given of fathers, of the life and honesty of clerks; that forbid that a clerk be no merchant, that he be no usurer, that he be no hunter, that he be no common player, that he bear no weapon; the laws that forbid clerks to haunt taverns, that forbid them to have suspect familiarity with women; the laws that command soberness, and a measurableness in apparel, and temperance in adorning of the body.

Let be rehearsed also to my lords these monks, canons and religious men, the laws that command them to go the strait way that leadeth unto Heaven, leaving the broad way of the world . . .

Above all things, let the laws be rehearsed that pertain and concern you, my reverend fathers and lords bishops, laws of your just and canonical election, in the chapters of your churches, with the calling of the Holy Ghost. For because that is not done nowadays, and because prelates are chosen oftentimes more by favour of men than by the grace of God; therefore truly have we not a few times bishops full little spiritual men, rather worldly than heavenly, savouring more the spirit of this world than the spirit of Christ.

Let the laws be rehearsed of the residence of bishops in their dioceses, that command that they look diligently, and take heed to the health of souls . . .

At the last let be renewed those laws and constitutions of fathers of the celebration of councils, that command provincial councils to be oftener used for the reformation of the Church . . .

The clergy and the spiritual parts once reformed in the Church, then may we with a just order proceed to the reformation of the lay part; the which truly will be very easy to do if we first be reformed.

From the sermon of John Colet, Dean of St Paul's, preached at the opening of Convocation in February, 1512

### D   A pre-Reformation bishop
I am well minded to promote Master Fisher your confessor to a bishopric and I assure you, madam, for none other cause but for the great and singular virtue that I know and see in him as well in cunning and natural wisdom and specially for his good and virtuous living and conversation; and by the promotion of such a man I know well it should encourage many other to live virtuously and to take such ways as he doth, which should be a good example to many other hereafter . . . I have in my days promoted many a man unadvisedly and I would now make some recompense to promote some good and virtuous man which I doubt not should best please God.

Henry VII to his mother Lady Margaret Beaufort, 1504

### E   A 'Holy Maid' at Leominster, Herefordshire
I remember me now what a work I have heard of that was at Leominster in the King's father's days, where the prior brought privily a strange wench into the church that said she was sent thither by God and would not lie out of the church [but] . . . in the rood loft where it was believed that she lived without any meat or drink, only by angels' food. And divers times she was [given communion] in sight of the people. . . .

5

There was a device with a small hair that conveyed the host from the paten of the chalice out of the prior's hands into her mouth as though it came alone, so that all the people not of the town only but also of the country about took her for a very quick saint and daily sought so thick to see her that many that could not come near to her cried out aloud 'Holy maiden Elizabeth, help me' and were fain to throw their offering over their fellows' head. . . . Now lay the prior with holy maiden Elizabeth nightly in the rood loft till she was after taken out and tried in the keeping by my lady the King's mother. And by the longing for meat, with voidance of that she had eaten (which had no saintly savour), she was perceived for no saint and confessed the whole matter.

'In faith,' quoth I, 'it had been great alms the prior and she had been burned together at one stake. What came of the prior?'

Quoth he, 'That I cannot tell. . . . But as for holy Elizabeth, I heard she lived and fared well and was a common harlot at Calais many a fair day after, where she laughed at the matter full merrily.'

From Thomas More: *Dialogue Concerning Heresies* (1529)

### F Pastoral guidance on prayer
. . . it is more speedful and meritable to you to say your Pater Noster in English than in such Latin as ye doth. For when ye speaketh in English, then ye know and understand well what ye say.

From John Mirk: *Festial* (A collection of sermons, *c.*1400)

### G Christ teaching the Lord's Prayer to the Apostles [from the *Arte or Crafte to Lyve Well* (1505)]

## H   An attack on pilgrimages in 1543

As it chanced one day Testwood to walk in the church at afternoon, and to behold the pilgrims, especially of Devonshire and Cornwall, how they came in by plumps, with candles and images of wax in their hands, to offer to good king Henry [VI] of Windsor, as they called him, it pitied his heart to see such great idolatry committed, and how vainly the people had spent their goods in coming so far to kiss a spur, and to have an old hat set upon their heads . . . he admonished them so long, till at last his words, as God would, took such place in some of them, that they said, they never would go a pilgrimage more.

. . . Now were many offended with Testwood; the canons for speaking against their profit; the wax-sellers for hindering their market.

John Foxe: *Acts and Monuments (Book of Martyrs)* (1563)

## I   A parish church in London

The parish church of St Andrew Undershaft . . . which hath been new builded by parishioners there, since the year 1520, every man putting to his helping hand, some with their purses, other with their bodies: Steven Gennings, merchant Tailor, sometime Mayor of London, caused at his charges to be builded the whole north side of the great middle aisle, both of the body and quire, as appeareth by his arms over every pillar graven, and also the north aisle, which he roofed with timber and ceiled, also the whole south side of the church was glassed, and the pews of the south chapel made of his costs, as appeareth in every window and upon the said pews. He deceased in the year 1524 and was buried in the Grey Friars' church.

From John Stow: *A Survey of London* (1603)

## J   A parish community in York

Of your charity, pray for the soul of Christopher Seel, Chanter of the Church of York, and sometime Clerk of the Works: of whose devotion the window was glazed in the year of our Lord God 1537.

Of your great charity pray for the souls of Martin Sosa, he was sometime Sheriff of York and goldsmith, born in Spain, and Ellen his wife, who caused this window to be made of his costs and charges.

Of your charity pray for the soul of Mr Thomas Marsar, sometime clerk of St Peter's works, in whose time this church was new erect and builded, and of his devotion caused this window to be glazed with his own costs and charges. AD 1535.

Of your charity, pray for the souls of William Beckwith and Jane his wife . . . Beckwith and Ann his wife, which caused this window to be glazed. AD 1530.

Inscriptions from the windows in the north and south aisles of the church of St Michael-le-Belfry (recorded in the seventeenth century)

## K   The nave of Cirencester parish church, built 1516–30

## L  Evidence from wills

I, Thomas Foldyngton of Barholm. My body to be buried in the chapel of Our Blessed Lady within the parish church of St Martin in Barholm, to the reparation of which I bequeath vjs. viijd. . . . To Joan Day my daughter [land] and she for that same to keep the lights before the image of Our Lady in the church of Barholm as I have done in times past. . . . Also to the foresaid Joan [certain land] and for that same to offer every year during her life in the parish church of Barholm the Thursday in the first whole week of Lent iiij mass pennies and to give to the ringers a pennyworth of bread and a gallon of ale. . . . To my Lady of Lincoln vjd. To my curate the vicar of Barholm my best quick goods for to pray for my soul and set my name in his bead roll. To the high altar for tithes negligently forgotten half a seme barley. To the Sepulchre light half a seme barley. To the reparation of the bell viijd. To the Trinity light viijd. To the reparation of the church of Barholm ijs. To the convent of the abbey in Bourne to pray for my soul iijs. iiijd. To the church of Barholm a blue cloth to bear over the sacrament upon Corpus Christi day and other times convenient. To the church of Stow iijs. iiijd. . . . To the iiij. orders of friars in Stamford, each of the orders vs., to sing or cause to be done for my soul and them that I am bound to pray for and all Christian souls ij. trentals, that is for to say each of the foresaid orders half a trental.

From the will of Thomas Foldyngton, 22 June 1530

# Questions

1 Roy and Barlow were both ex-Franciscans who had to write in exile. How does this affect the value of Source B as historical evidence?

(5 marks)

2 Compare Sources C and D as evidence for the quality of the clergy in the pre-Reformation Church. (6 marks)

3 What does Source E tell us about the strengths and weaknesses of the pre-Reformation Church in England? (7 marks)

4 Read the extract from *Acts and Monuments* in Source H (John Foxe was a committed Protestant).
  a According to Foxe, why did people criticise Testwood? (2 marks)
  b Why do you think Foxe chose to mention these particular criticisms? (3 marks)
  c How valuable do you consider this account to be for the student of pre-Reformation religion in England? (5 marks)

5   What can we learn from Sources I and J about the parish community
    in the pre-Reformation Church?                          **(7 marks)**

6   With reference to Source L, analyse the usefulness of wills in assessing
    attitudes towards religion.                             **(7 marks)**

7   '. . . the consensus of recent historians, that pre-Reformation religion
    was a flourishing faith is amply confirmed' (Ronald Hutton). To what
    extent do these sources support this statement?         **(8 marks)**

# 2 HENRY VIII'S REFORMATION

The events of the 1530s had made necessary some definite statement on the doctrine of the English Church [A-E]. The King's rejection of the Pope's authority, his treatment of the monasteries and his support of known reformers caused uncertainty as to what could or could not be taught from the pulpit and believed by the faithful. Official declarations were closely examined for any shifts in emphasis or changes in wording that could be brought in to support a particular interpretation.

What were the influences that contributed to these statements? In the first place there were Henry's own religious convictions [D]. Even after separation from Rome, he remained committed to a variety of traditional practices and beliefs [F-I], such as clerical celibacy or the saying of masses for the dead, but at other times he showed definite signs of radicalism and unorthodox interpretation.

However, he did not form his opinions in isolation and, according to Thomas Cranmer, it was usual for Henry to rely on others to read books for him and get his ideas at second hand. There is debate over the extent to which Henry could be influenced by others. At one extreme he is seen as a tool in the hands of his ministers and courtiers [J-K]; at the other, he is totally in control and following his own counsel. It is a debate that has a bearing on his religious policy. For much of the 1530s, Henry's most successful servants seemed to be those of the reforming 'party' – the likes of Cranmer and Cromwell. These were the men who had solved the marriage problem and given Henry a new role in the Church. There were also conservatives like the Duke of Norfolk or Bishops Gardiner and Tunstal who could lead an effective action on behalf of traditional beliefs while not challenging the royal supremacy.

What notice did Henry have to take of popular feeling, whether it was expressed in as forceful a way as the Pilgrimage of Grace or more peacefully through bishops' reports from their dioceses?

Finally, the demands of foreign policy might also be taken into account [L-M]. What approach should be taken when negotiating with German Lutherans and to what extent did the Catholic powers require some conciliation?

As for the doctrine itself, what kind of Church did Henry set up? Would it be more accurate to define it as Catholic or Protestant? How was it able to satisfy both Gardiner and Cranmer, or did it in fact satisfy neither of them?

### A Some instructions for preachers

*Item.* Also to forfend that no preachers for a year, shall preach neither with nor against Purgatory, honouring of saints, that priests may have wives, that faith only justifieth, to go on pilgrimages, to forge miracles, considering these things have caused dissension amongst the subjects of this realm already, which thanked be God is now pacified.

*Item.* That from henceforth all preachers shall purely, sincerely and justly preach the scripture and word of Christ, and not mix them with man's institutions, nor make men believe that the force of God's law and man's law is like; nor that any man is able or hath power to dispense with God's law.

An Order for Preaching, 1535

### B Part of the First Statement on Doctrine issued on Henry's authority

... we being of late to our great regret, credibly advertised of such diversity in opinions, as have grown and sprung in this our realm, as well concerning certain articles necessary to our salvation, as also touching certain other honest and commendable ceremonies, rites, and usages now of long time used and accustomed in our churches ... have not only in our own person at many times taken great pains, study, labours, and travails, but also have caused our bishops, and other the most discreet and best learned men of our clergy of this our whole realm, to be assembled in our convocation, for the full debatement and quiet determination of the same. ...

As touching the sacrament of the altar ... they ought and must constantly believe, that under the form and figure of bread and wine, which we there presently do see and perceive by outward senses, is verily, substantially, and really contained and comprehended the very selfsame body and blood of our Saviour Jesus Christ. ...

As touching the order and cause of our justification ... sinners attain this justification by contrition and faith with charity ... not as though our contrition, or faith, or any works proceeding thereof, can worthily merit or deserve to attain the said justification; for the only mercy and grace of the Father, promised freely unto us for His Son's sake, Jesu Christ, and the merits of His blood and passion, be the only sufficient and worthy causes thereof; and yet that notwithstanding ... although acceptation to everlasting life be conjoined with justification, yet our good works be necessarily required to the attaining of everlasting life; and we being justified, be necessarily bound, and it is our necessary duty to do good works. ...

As touching images ... first that there may be attributed to them, that they be representers of virtue and good example, and that they also be by occasion the kindlers and stirrers of men's minds, and make men oft to remember and lament their sins and offences, especially the images of Christ and Our Lady; and that therefore it is meet that they should stand in the churches. . . . And as for the censing of them and kneeling and offering to them . . . the people ought to be diligently taught that they in no wise do it, nor think it meet to be done to the same images, but only to be done to God, and in his honour although it be done before the images, whether it be of Christ, of the Cross, of Our Lady, or of any other saint beside. . . .

As touching praying to the saints . . . albeit grace, remission of sin, and salvation, cannot be obtained but of God only by the mediation of our Saviour Christ, which is only sufficient Mediator for our sins: yet it is very laudable to pray to saints in Heaven everlastingly living, whose charity is ever permanent, to be intercessors, and to pray for us and with us, unto Almighty God. . . .

As concerning the rites and ceremonies of Christ's Church, as to have such vestments in doing God's service, as be and have been most part used, as sprinkling of holy water . . . giving of holy bread . . . bearing of candles on Candlemas-day in memory of Christ the Spiritual Light . . . giving of ashes on Ash Wednesday, to put in remembrance every Christian man in the beginning of Lent and penance, that he is but ashes and earth . . . bearing of palms on Palm-Sunday, in memory of the receiving of Christ into Jerusalem . . . creeping to the cross, and humbling ourselves to Christ on Good Friday before the cross . . . setting up the sepulchre of Christ, whose body after his death was buried; the hallowing of the font, and other like exorcisms and benedictions by the ministers of Christ's Church; and all other like laudable customs, rites and ceremonies be not to be contemned and cast away, but to be used and continued as things good and laudable, to put us in remembrance of those spiritual things that they do signify. . . . But none of these ceremonies have power to remit sin, but only to stir and lift up our minds unto God, by whom only our sins be forgiven.

From the Ten Articles, 1536

## C  Henry's introduction to the bishops' book (1537) [a definition of doctrine signed by the bishops]

Albeit that hitherto we have had no time convenient to overlook your great painstaking in the long search and diligent debating of this your book . . . much less time to pound and weigh such things as you therein have written: yet, according to your suit and petition, we have caused your said book to be printed, and will the same to be conveyed into all the parts of our realm, nothing doubting but that you, being men of such learning and virtue, as we know you to be, have indeed performed in the whole work that you do promise in the preface. . . . We nothing mislike your judgement, so that ye have in such wise handled those places that every man may know both his whole duty towards God . . . and also know how he hath to govern himself in this political life, as a utile member of the same, and also towards God's ministers, the heads and governors of states, and towards his neighbours, much better than they have done heretofore. Notwithstanding that we are otherwise occupied, we have taken as it were a taste of this your book, and found therein nothing but that is both meet to come from you, and also worthy our praise and commendation.

From *The Godly and Pious Institution of a Christian Man* (1537)

### D   An example of Henry's later response to the book [Henry added the underlined words to the original text]
And I believe that by this passion and death of our saviour Jesu Christ, I doing my duty, not only my corporal death is so destroyed that it shall never have power to hurt me, but rather it is made wholesome and profitable unto me. . . .

The penitent must conceive certain hope and faith that God will forgive him his sins and repute him justified . . . not only for the worthiness of any merit or work done by the penitent but chiefly for the only merits of the blood and passion of our saviour Christ.

Quoted in J. Scarisbrick: *Henry VIII* (1968)

### E   An attempt to settle disputed doctrine by an act of Parliament
First, that in the most blessed sacrament of the altar . . . is present really, under the form of bread and wine, the natural body and blood of our Saviour Jesu Christ, conceived of the Virgin Mary, and that after the consecration there remaineth no substance of bread and wine, nor any other substance but the substance of Christ, God and man;

Secondly, that communion in both kinds is not necessary ad salutem by the law of God to all persons, and it is to be believed and not doubted of, but that in the flesh under form of bread is the very blood, and with the blood under form of wine is the very flesh, as well apart as though they were both together;

From An Act abolishing diversity in opinions (Act of Six Articles), 1539

### F   Maintaining orthodoxy
In the same parliament, too, the king published a general, or, so to speak, an universal pardon, by which he forgave the nobility and others of his subjects all heresies, treasons, felonies, with many other offences against the laws and statutes of the realm, committed before the 1st July 1540. . . .

Many . . . of the nobility were excepted from this pardon; among whom was the popish bishop of Chichester, and a man of the name of Wilson (who had, on a former occasion, been pardoned by the king, and set at liberty after two years' imprisonment for his support of the pope), together with some other priests, who, as they maintained the supremacy of the pope, would not admit the king's title, wherein he styles himself 'supreme head of the church of England'. All anabaptists too were excepted, and sacramentaries, as they are called, and all those who do not admit transubstantiation . . .

Soon after the dissolution of parliament, namely on the 30th July last year, were executed six of those men who had been excepted from the general pardon. Three of them were popish priests, whose names were Abel, Powell, and Fetherston, and who refused to acknowledge the king's new title, and his authority over the clergy. . . . The remaining three were preachers of the gospel [i.e. reformers] and of no mean order; their name were Barnes, Gerrard and Jerome. . . . I could never ascertain, though I have made diligent enquiry, the true reason why these three gospellers were excepted from the general pardon; so that I can conjecture none more likely, than that the king, desiring to gratify the clergy and the ignorant and rude mob, together with the obstinate part of his nobility and citizens, appointed these three victims, as he probably considered them, as it were for a holocaust, to appease those parties, or to acquire fresh popularity with them.

From a letter from the Protestant reformer Richard Hilles to Henry Bullinger, 1541

## G  Prohibiting heretical books

The king's most excellent majesty, understanding how under pretense of expounding and declaring the truth of God's Scripture, divers lewd and evil-disposed persons have taken occasion to utter and sow abroad, by books imprinted in the English tongue, sundry pernicious and detestable errors and heresies, not only contrary to the laws of this realm, but also repugnant to the true sense of God's law and his word. . . . His highness, minding to foresee the dangers that might ensue thereof . . . is enforced to use his general prohibition, commandment, and proclamation as followeth:

. . . that from henceforth no man, woman, or other person, of what estate, condition, or degree soever he or they be, shall after the last day of August next ensuing, receive, take, have, or keep in his or their possession, the text of the New Testament of Tyndale's or Coverdale's translation in English, nor any other than is permitted by the act of parliament . . . nor after the said day shall receive, have, take, or keep in his or their possession any manner of book printed or written in the

English tongue which be or shall be set forth in the names of Frith, Tyndale, Wycliff, Joy, Roy, Basille, Bale, Barnes, Coverdale, Turner, Tracy, or by any of them, or any other book or books containing matter contrary to the king's majesty's book called A Necessary Doctrine and Erudition for any Christian Man . . .

From a Royal Proclamation issued in July, 1546

### H   John Bale's account of the examination of Anne Askew, tried and executed for heresy in 1546 [Anne Askew's words are interspersed with comments by Bale]

(Askew) Thirdly, he asked wherefore I said that I had rather read five lines in the Bible than to hear five masses in the temple. I confessed that I said no less: not for the dispraise of either the epistle or the gospel; but because the one did greatly edify me, and the other nothing at all. . . .

(Bale) A commandment hath Christ given us to search the holy scriptures . . . But of the Latin popish mass is not one word in all the Bible, and therefore it pertaineth not to the faith. . . .

(Askew) Sixthly, he asked me what I said to the king's book. And I answered him, that I could say nothing to it, because I never saw it.

(Bale) All crafty ways possible sought this crafty questmonger, or else the devil in him, to bring this poor innocent lamb to the slaughter-place of antichrist. Much after this sort sought the wicked Pharisees, by certain of their own faction, or hired satellites, with the Herodians, to bring Christ in danger of Caesar, and so have him slain. . . .

(Askew) Then would they needs know if I would deny the sacrament to be Christ's body and blood. I said, Yea; for the same Son of God that was born of the Virgin Mary, is now glorious in heaven, and will come again from thence, at the latter day, like as he went up. . . . And as for that ye call your God, is but a piece of bread. For a more proof thereof (mark it when ye list) let it lie in the box but three months, and it will be mould, and so turn to nothing that is good. Whereupon I am persuaded that it cannot be God.

(Bale) Christ Jesus, the eternal Son of God, was condemned . . . for a seditious heretic . . . and suffered death for it . . . by the law then used. Is it, then, any marvel if his inferior subject here, and faithful member, do the same. . . . But how that dry and corruptible cake of theirs should become a god, many men wonder nowadays, in the light of the gospel, like as they have done aforetime also. . . .

From John Bale's account of the examination of Anne Askew, 1546

## I  Title page from John Bale's account of Anne Askew's examination, 1546

The first examinacy=
on of Anne Askewe, latelye mar
tyred in Smythfelde, by the Ro=
myshe popes vpholders, with
the Elucydacyon of
Johan Bale.

Sauoure is disceytfull/and bewtye is a vay
ne thynge. But a woman that feareth the
lorde/is worthye to be praysed. She ope=
neth her mouthe to wysdome/and in her lan
guage is the lawe of grace. Prouerb. xxxj.

## J  A letter on Anne Boleyn

And as I loved her not a little for the love which I judged her to bear towards God and his gospel; so if she prove culpable there is not one that loveth God and his gospel that ever will favour her . . . and God hath sent her this punishment, for that she feignedly hath professed his gospel in her mouth and not in heart and deed. . . . I trust that your grace will bear no less entire favour unto the truth of the gospel, than you did before; forasmuch as your grace's favour to the gospel was not led by affection unto her but by zeal unto the truth.

Thomas Cranmer to Henry VIII on the fall of Anne Boleyn, May 1536

## K  A letter on Anne of Cleves

On the 12th of January I received letters from our English brethren. . . . The state and condition of that kingdom is much more sound and healthy since the marriage of the queen, than it was before. She is an excellent woman, and one who fears God: great hopes are entertained of a very extensive propagation of the gospel by her influence.

John Butler to Henry Bullinger, Basle, 24 February 1540

### L   Religion and foreign policy in 1546

Whilst the said bishop of Winchester was now remaining beyond the seas ... the king's majesty and the said archbishop [Cranmer] having conference together for the reformation of some superstitious enormities in the church, amongst other things the king determined forthwith to pull down the roods in every church and to suppress the accustomed ringing on Allhallow-night, with a few such like vain ceremonies ... [Later] when Master Denny had moved the king thereunto, the king made this answer:

   'I am now otherwise resolved, for you shall send my lord of Canterbury word, that since I spoke with him about these matters, I have received letters from my lord of Winchester, now being on the other side of the sea, about the conclusion of a league between us, the emperor and the French king, and he writeth plainly unto us, that the league will not prosper nor go forward, if we make any other innovation, change or alteration either in religion or ceremonies, than heretofore hath already been commenced and done. Wherefore my lord of Canterbury must take patience herein and forbear until we may espy a more apt and convenient time for that purpose.'

John Foxe: *Acts and Monuments (Book of Martyrs)* (1563)

### M   Further insight into Henry's foreign policy [the following incident was reported by Cranmer to his secretary in Edward VI's reign]

'I am sure you were at Hampton Court,' quoth the archbishop, 'when the French king's ambassador was entertained there at those solemn banqueting-houses, not long before the king's death; namely, when, after the banquet was done the first night, the king was leaning upon the ambassador and upon me: if I should tell what communication between the king's highness and the said ambassador was had, concerning the establishing of sincere religion then, a man would hardly have believed it: nor had I myself thought the king's highness had been so forward in those matters as then appeared. I may tell you, it passed the pulling down of roods, and suppressing the ringing of bells. I take it that few in England would have believed, that the king's majesty and the French king had been, at this point, not only, within half a year after, to have changed the mass in both the realms into a communion (as we now use it), but also utterly to have extirpated and banished the bishop of Rome, and his usurped power, out of both their realms and dominions. Yea, they were so thoroughly and firmly resolved in that behalf, that they meant also to exhort the emperor to do the like in Flanders and other his countries and seigniories; or else they would break off from him. And herein the king's highness willed me,' quoth the archbishop, 'to pen a form thereof to be sent to the French king to consider of. But the deep and most secret providence of Almighty God, owing to this realm a sharp scourge for our iniquities, prevented for a time this their most godly device and intent, by taking to his mercy both these princes.'

From John Foxe: *Acts and Monuments (Book of Martyrs)* (1563)

# Questions

**1 a** According to Source A, what problem faced the English Church in the mid-1530s? **(2 marks)**

  **b** How is the second item in Source A relevant to the annulment of Henry VIII's marriage to Catherine of Aragon? **(2 marks)**

**2** How useful are Sources F and G in showing how serious a problem heresy was in the reign of Henry VIII? **(6 marks)**

**3 a** In what ways does Source E 'tighten up' the doctrine of the Eucharist expressed in Source B? **(2 marks)**

  **b** Why would Anne Askew's argument on the Eucharist in Source H not have convinced her accusers? **(3 marks)**

**4 a** How does Source I reflect the attitude of John Bale to Anne Askew and her beliefs? **(5 marks)**

  **b** Comment on John Bale's use of language in Source H. **(4 marks)**

**5** Comment on the significance of the letters in Sources J and K. **(6 marks)**

**6** 'Henry died a Catholic, though a rather bad Catholic' (Haig). To what extent do these sources support such an assessment of Henry VIII? **(8 marks)**

# 3 THE DISSOLUTION OF THE MONASTERIES

It was not just monasteries that were dissolved. The phrase 'dissolution of the monasteries' also refers to friaries, houses of canons and nunneries, many of which had for centuries been an integral part of English society. By the early sixteenth century there were almost 800 religious houses in England, some of them possessing enormous wealth and others with only a handful of inmates and a meagre income [A-D].

What was the purpose of these foundations? First of all, they provided a spiritual service, praying for the world at large, both living and dead. How effective they were in this is of course impossible to measure. In addition, they also provided 'social services' of varying kinds – charity, hospitality, education – but with little consistency from one place to another [A, D]. Robert Aske, leader of the Pilgrimage of Grace, spoke of these twin functions when he lamented the passing of the abbeys, but he was speaking only of the north of England and in justification of his rebellion. Not everyone was as enthusiastic as Aske. There is some evidence from dwindling bequests that the abbeys had declined in popularity, but even so the bequests continued up until their last years and the major houses at least had little difficulty in recruiting new members.

In assessing the attitude to the religious houses in the sixteenth century it might be useful to compare them to the cathedrals and parish churches of the Church of England today. A significant minority work or worship in them on a regular basis; but a much larger section of the population accepts them as part of the fabric of society, attends occasionally, expects them to be there and will make the occasional contribution to their upkeep. Frequently any criticisms are not against the existence of the institutions themselves but are comments on unspecified wealth, not conforming to traditional ideals or not being relevant enough to modern society (sometimes both at the same time), or dissatisfaction with particular individuals.

The dissolution itself poses a number of questions. Why was it undertaken in the first place? Was it purely for financial reasons? The spoils of the dissolution had the potential to make Henry VIII a very rich king indeed, although many historians think that better use could have been made of them. What role did religion play? To close some of the religious houses could be seen as the act of a sincere though conservative reformer who still valued monastic life but wanted to see its old ideals restored [A]. To close all of them, however, could be seen as the act of a more radical reformer, convinced that any form of monastic life was a perversion of true religion [M]. Where did Henry stand and just how calculated was he in pursuing his policy? Did he plan it all from the beginning or did he take advantage of each success to move one step further?

Henry was not the only one to gain [I]. Whether they were long-term critics of monasticism or simply accepted what they could not prevent, many individuals were willing to benefit from gifts, leases of land and the sale of items which could be removed [J-L]. People expanded their fortunes to such an extent with the profits from the dissolution that allowing them to keep their newly acquired monastic lands was the only concession that Cardinal Pole had to make when he was sent to reconcile England to the Roman Catholic Church in Mary I's reign.

## A   An early example of dissolution

Licence for John, bishop of Ely, to expel the prioress and nuns from the convent of St Radegunde, which is of the foundation and patronage of the bishop and which has become reduced to poverty and decay by reason of the dissolute conduct and incontinence of the prioress and nuns, on account of their vicinity to the University of Cambridge, so that they cannot maintain divine service, hospitality or other works of mercy and piety . . . [and] are reduced to two in number, one of whom is professed elsewhere and the other is an infant, and to found a college in its stead for one master, six fellows and a certain number of scholars to be instructed in grammar, to pray and celebrate divine service daily for the king, his queen Elizabeth . . . and for the soul of the king's father Edmund Earl of Richmond; the college to be called the College of St Mary the Virgin, St John the Evangelist and St Radegunde the Virgin by Cambridge . . .

Licence granted to the bishop of Ely, 12 June 1497

**B** The abbey church at Gloucester [given cathedral status after the dissolution, in 1541]

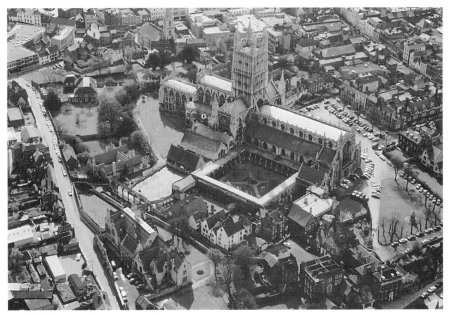

**C** The bell-tower of Evesham Abbey, built by Abbot Lichfield some time between 1524 and 1532

## D   Letters from the Commissioners

### (i) Thomas Bedyll to Thomas Cromwell, 15 January 1536

In my most hearty wise I commend me to you, doing you to understand that I am now at Ramsey, where in mine opinion the abbot and convent be as true and faithful obedientiaries to the king's grace as any religious folks in this realm, and live as uprightly as any other, after the best sort of living that has been among religious folks this many years, that is to say more given to ceremonies than is necessary. I pray God I may find other houses in no worse condition, and then I will be right glad that I took this journey.

### (ii) George Giffard to Thomas Cromwell, 19 June 1536

And, sir, forasmuch as of late my fellows and I did write unto Mr Chancellor of the Augmentations in favour of the abbey of St James and the nunnery of Catesby in Northamptonshire, which letter he showed to the King's highness in the favour of these houses, where the King's highness was displeased, as he said to my servant Thomas Harper, saying that it was like that we had received rewards, which caused us to write as we did.

### (iii) Richard Layton to Thomas Cromwell, 4 June 1537

Please it you to understand that whereas ye intend shortly to visit, and be like shall have many suitors unto you for the same to be your commissioners, if it might stand in your pleasure that Doctor Lee and I might have committed unto us the north country. . . . There is neither monastery, cell, priory, nor any other religious house in the north but either Doctor Lee or I have familiar acquaintance within x or xij miles of it, so that no knavery can be hid from us in that country. . . . If ye had leisure to overlook the book of articles that I made for your visitation this time xij months, and to mark every sundry interrogatory therein written, doubtless there is matter sufficient to detect and open all coloured sanctity, all superstitious rules of pretensed religion and other abuses detestable of all sorts, hitherto cloaked and coloured by the reformers (so named) of every [religious order] which ever, by friendship, till this day hath found crafty means to be their own visitors, thereby no reformation intending neither good religion (if any be) to increase, but only to keep secret all matters of mischief, with much privy murmering among themselves, selling their jewels and plate to take half the value for ready money, with great ruin and decay of their houses, which must needs yet continue and endure daily more and with increase, unless ye now set to your helping hand . . .

## E   A petition to Cromwell

With due reverence I commend me unto your honourable lordship, humbly ascertaining the same that I send your lordship by this bearer part of our fen fish, right meekly beseeching your lordship favourably to accept the same fish and to be a good and favourable lord unto me and my poor house, in such cause as I hereafter shall have cause to sue unto your good lordship, and I with my brethren shall daily pray to our Lord God for the long continuance of your good lordship in health.

The Abbot of Croyland to Thomas Cromwell, 25 March 1537

### F   The surrender of the abbeys

... forasmuch as I am informed that your lordship intendeth to depose the prior of the Charterhouse within the Isle of Axholme, this shall be to desire you to permit the said prior still to continue in his room, for I am about, through the help of such friends as I have in those parts, to procure that the said prior shall willingly resign the same into the King's hands.

Thomas Cranmer to Thomas Cromwell, 7 March 1538

### G   Surrender resisted

My good lord, the truth is, I nor my said brethren have never consented to surrender our monastery, nor yet do, nor never will do by our good wills, unless it shall please the king's grace to give us commandment so to do, which I cannot perceive in the commission of Master Holcroft so to be. And if any information be given unto his majesty, or unto your good lordship, that we should consent to surrender, as is above said, I assure your good lordship, upon my fidelity and truth, there was never none such consent made by me nor my brethren, nor no person nor persons had authority so to do in our names ...

The Abbot of Vale Royal monastery to Thomas Cromwell, 9 September 1538

### H   Conditions for surrendering or continuing

Whereas certain governors and companies of a few religious houses have lately made free and voluntary surrenders into his grace's hands, his grace's highness has commanded me for your reposes ... to advertise you that unless there had been overtures made by the said houses that have resigned, his grace would never have retained the same and that his majesty intends not in any wise to trouble you or to devise for the suppression of any religious house that stands, except they shall either desire of themselves with one whole consent and forsake the same or else misuse themselves contrary to their allegiance. In which case, they shall deserve the loss of much more than their houses and possessions, that is the loss also of their lives. Wherefore, in this you may repose yourselves, giving yourselves to serve God devoutly, to live like true and faithful subjects to his majesty, and to provide honestly for the sustentation of your houses and the relieving of poor people with the hospitality of the same, without consumption and wilful waste and spoil of things that has been lately made in many abbeys, as though the governors of them minded only their dissolution.

... And if any man, of what degree soever he shall be, pronounce anything to the contrary hereof, fail you not either to apprehend him if you shall be able or if he be such a personage as you shall not dare meddle with, to write to his majesty's highness their name or names and report that he or they so lewdly behaving themselves may be punished for the same as shall appertain.

Thomas Cromwell to an unknown abbot, March 1538

### I   The use of monastic resources

Little is known of what is concluded in Parliament, which has been engaged from the first in providing for the security of the realm, for which the king demands money, but they reply coldly enough. They are also discussing the reduction of certain abbeys of which they wish to make bishoprics, the foundation of schools for children, and hospitals for the poor ...

The French ambassador, Marillac, to Francis I, 20 May 1539

### J   Distributing monastic lands and fabric

I have bethought me that if I have not some piece of this suppressed land by purchase or gift of the king's majesty, I should stand out of the case of few men of worship of this realm. As God knows I was and am as glad as any man of this realm of the suppression of these orgulous persons and devourers of God's word and takers away of the glory of Christ, and I reckon before this they were takers away of the wealth of this realm and spies to the devilish bishop of Rome. And because my heirs shall be in the same mind for their own profit, I will gladly, if it might stand with the king's majesty's pleasure, buy certain parcels of this suppressed land in these parts, and I will send the king's majesty good sufficient sureties for the payment of his money, and sell part of my inheritance to pay part of the money in hand. ... Nor I do not this for no covetousness but to stand in the case of others.

Sir Richard Grenville to Thomas Cromwell, July 1539

### K   The motive of profit

I demanded of my father, thirty years after the suppression, which had bought part of the timber of the church and all the timber in the steeple, with the bell frame, with other his partners therein (in the which steeple hung eight, yea nine bells; whereof the least but one could not be bought at this day for £20, which bells I did see hang there myself, more than a year after the suppression) whether he thought well of the religious persons and of the religion then used. And he told me, 'Yea, for,' said he, 'I did see no cause to the contrary.' 'Well,' said I, 'then how came it to pass you was so ready to destroy and spoil the thing that you thought well of?' 'What should I do?' said he; 'Might I not as well as others have some profits of the spoil of the abbey? For I did see all would away; and therefore did as others did.'

Michael Sherbrook, writing about Roche Abbey, c.1591

## L   Profits from the dissolution

| The Grey Friars of Staff. surrendered | The sale of goods there made the xxvijth day of September, anno xxxᵐᵒ Henrici viij as hereafter followeth | |
|---|---|---|

| | | |
|---|---|---|
| ... sol. | Item, a table of alabaster standing in the church sold to Mr Loveson | 2s 8d |
| sol. | Item, in St Francis' chapel all the seats sold to Robert Doryngton | 4d |
| sol. | Item, a image of St Katherine, sold to Lee | 6d |
| | Item, sold to Robert Doryngton, old books and a coffer in the library | 2s |
| | Item, sold a pair of portative organs to Mr Besum | 2s |
| | Item, an old coffer in the vestry, sold to James Clement | 2s 8d |
| | Item, old wax, sold to Robert Doryngton | 4d |
| | Item, a lamp, sold to Robert Doryngton | 8d |
| | Item, old books in the vestry, sold to the same Robert | 8d |
| | Item, sold to Robert Whitgreve, a missal | 8d |
| | Item, 2 altar candlesticks and a pyx of copper, sold to Mr Swynnerton | 12d |

From the accounts of John Scudamore, the King's Receiver, 1539

## M   Henry VIII on the dissolution process [giving advice to be passed on to the Regent of Scotland]

... for the extirpation of the state of monks and friars, the enterprise whereof requireth politic handling, it shall be first necessary that the governor send substantial and faithful commissioners, as it were to put a good order in the same. . . . Which commissioners must have secret commission most secretly and groundly to examine all the religious of their conversation and behaviour in their livings, whereby if it be well handled, he shall get knowledge of all their abominations; and that once gotten, he [consult] with the chief of the noble men, agreeing with them for the distribution of some of the lands of the abbeys to be divided to himself and among them, which shall be to their great profit and benefit ... and then, with the bishops apart, or some such of them as be most tractable, and making unto them as assurance of their estate, should also offer unto them some augmentation by annexing to their small portions some of such small houses as lie conveniently for them, and also to devise with them for the alteration of certain other abbeys to the state of secular priests, with finding of poor lame men, of scholars to the university, as their portion may serve, whereby the state of the clergy shall be better preserved and in a more decent order than it is now in. And then with both parties, both bishops and temporal lords, to devise how necessary it is to allot a good portion of those lands of the abbeys to the augmentation of the state of the king and the young queen, and their heirs and successors, so as they may be able to maintain their estate upon the public revenues, and not enforced in times of peace to seek such ways as their late king did, whereby to grieve and annoy his people. And it is to be thought that the platform of the disposition of those abbeys being in this wise made and known before, particularly to what uses they should be employed as afore, with a reasonable provision for the entertainment of the religious men now being in them, and for the term of their lives, the proceeding to the execution in the suppression of the same, will be the more easy and facile among such as will understand the truth, and acknowledge the abominable life continued among those which now in diversities of sects usurp those places, not only to the high displeasure of God, but also as a great deformity in the commonwealth, spending their time in all idleness and filthiness with such face of hypocrisy and superstition as is intolerable.

Henry VIII to Sir Ralph Sadler, April 1543

# Questions

**1** Of what value are physical remains such as Sources B and C in the study of the dissolution? **(6 marks)**

**2** Using your own knowledge, explain the reference to the Court of Augmentations in Source D(ii). **(2 marks)**

**3 a** Compare Sources D(i), (ii) and (iii) in what they reveal about the attitudes of the commissioners involved in the dissolution process. **(5 marks)**

  **b** How reliable would you consider the findings of these commissioners to be? **(4 marks)**

**4** In the context of the dissolution comment on the significance and date of Source E. **(3 marks)**

# 4 HENRY VIII'S REFORMATION: OPPOSITION

Change will always provoke opposition. Henry VIII and his advisers were well aware of this and, as well as implementing their policies, set out to anticipate and to punish any active criticism of them, whether expressed in word or action. The printing-press and the pulpit, painters and playwrights were all used to try to win the people over to the new order. And when persuasion did not work, dissidents were sought out, examined and, where necessary, punished [E]. Reports came in to Cromwell from all over the country detailing minor incidents such as the prior at Droitwich, Worcestershire, who had not erased the Pope's name from the service books or the Suffolk parson who insisted on celebrating the feast of Thomas Becket.

Opposition came in many different forms and from many different quarters [B, F]. John Fisher, Bishop of Rochester, and Sir Thomas More, once the Lord Chancellor, were executed in 1535 [D]. They seemed to be isolated though eminent individuals and it was perhaps their very eminence that caused their downfall. Two such examples would serve Henry very well for persuasion and intimidation. But although they are probably the most well-known, there are other examples. Critics expressed themselves in Parliament and even at court there were those who were half-hearted in pursuing some of the more radical policies. Throughout the country priests and lay people voiced their dissatisfaction [I]. In the Pilgrimage of Grace [G-H] opposition went beyond words to armed demonstration and for a few months Henry faced a serious challenge to his position.

What caused this opposition? More and Fisher refused the supremacy. [C], others defended aspects of their traditional religion. The Pilgrimage of Grace was apparently sparked off by the dissolution of the monasteries, but some historians would prefer to see it as courtly faction politics transferred to a regional uprising. To what extent did religion and politics become entangled? There are signs also that the way in which the reforms were effected and the way in which the central government seemed to be interfering in local life caused unhappiness. And some parliamentary critics feared that the response from other countries would have an adverse affect on English trade.

But ultimately the opposition was unsuccessful. Was the tradition of loyalty and obedience too strong to be overcome? Henry proceeded gradually with his reformation – at what point should one start to resist the process? Should one resist at all? Surely the King knew best? After all, he did have the bishops and universities on his side.

## A   The Emperor's interest

I have sent to tell the Chancellor [Sir Thomas More] that I have letters for him from your Majesty, and I wished to visit him. He begged me for the honour of God to forbear, for although he had given already sufficient proof of his loyalty that he ought to incur no suspicion, whoever came to visit him, yet, considering the time, he ought to abstain from everything which might provoke suspicion; and if there were no other reason, such a visitation might deprive him of the liberty which he had always used in speaking boldly in those matters which concerned your Majesty and the Queen [Catherine of Aragon]. He said he would not hold them in less regard than his life, not only out of the respect which is due to your Majesty and the Queen, but also for the welfare, honour, and conscience of his master, and the repose of his kingdom. With regard to the letter he begged me earnestly that I would keep it as it is till some other time, for if he received it he must communicate it, and he hoped a more propitious time would come for its acceptance, begging me to assure you of his most affectionate service.

The Imperial ambassador, Chapuys, to Charles V, 2 April 1531

## B   Organising opposition

About six or seven years ago [Throckmorton] conversed with Sir Thomas Dyngley in the garden at St John's about the Parliament matters. Dyngley wondered that the Act of Appeals should pass so lightly, and Throckmorton said it was no wonder as few would displease my lord Privy Seal [Cromwell]. Told Sir Thomas that he had been sent for by the King after speaking about that Act, and that he saw his Grace's conscience was troubled about having married his brother's wife. 'And I said to him that I told your Grace I feared if ye did marry Queen Anne your conscience would be more troubled at length, for it is thought ye have meddled both with the mother and the sister.' And his Grace said, 'Never with the mother.' And my lord Privy Seal standing by said, 'Nor never with the sister either, and therefore put that out of your mind.' This was in substance all their communication. Intended no harm to the King but only out of vainglory to show he was one that durst speak for the common wealth . . .

Was asked by my lord Privy Seal to write what other communication he may have had about the King at the Queen's Head or elsewhere; which is very hard for him to do. Reported the same conversation to Sir Thomas Englefield at Serjeants Inn, and, he believes, to Sir William

Essex; also, he rather thinks, to Sir William Barentyne. Essex, Barentyne, Sir John Gyfforde, Sir Marmaduke Constable and others did much use the Queen's Head at dinner and supper. Caused all servants to withdraw when they conversed of Parliament matters, but made no appointments to meet . . .

Just before that Parliament [of 1529] friar Peto, who was in a tower in Lambeth over the gate, sent for him and showed him two sermons that he and another friar had made before the King at Greenwich, and reported a long conversation he had had with the King in the garden after the sermon. He said he had told the King that he could have no other wife while the Princess Dowager lived. . . . He moreover advised [Throckmorton] if he were in Parliament house to stick to that matter as he would save his soul. Shortly after the beginning of the Parliament, when he had 'reasoned' to the Bill of Appeals, Sir Thomas More, then Chancellor, sent Saye for him to come and speak with him in the Parliament chamber. . . . Sir Thomas said that he was glad to hear that he was so good a Catholic and that, if he continued, he would deserve great reward of God and thanks at length of the King. [Throckmorton] took so much pride of this that he went shortly after to the bishop of Rochester with whom he had much conversation about the Acts of Appeals, Annates and Supremacy, and the authority given by our Lord to Peter. The last time he was with him the bishop gave him a book of his own device on the subject; which book he delivered to my lord Privy Seal at his house at Austin Friars. The bishop also advised him to speak with Mr Wilson, which he did at St Thomas the Apostle's, who also showed him divers books noted with his own hand, to confirm the same opinion. Went afterwards to Syon to one Reynolds, of whom he was confessed, and showed him his conscience in all these causes; who advised him to stick to his opinion to the death, else he would surely be damned, and also not to hold his peace in Parliament even if he thought his speaking could not prevail. This was against the opinion of the bishop of Rochester and Mr Wilson, but Reynolds said he did not know how he might encourage others in the house to do the same.

From the summary of a letter from Sir George Throckmorton to Henry VIII, 1537

### C  Cranmer offers his advice on Fisher and More

Right worshipful Master Cromwell . . . I doubt not but you do right well remember, that my lord of Rochester and master More were contented to be sworn to the act of the king's succession, but not to the preamble of the same. What was the cause of their refusal thereof, I am uncertain, and they would by no means express the same. Nevertheless it must needs be, either the diminution of the authority of the bishop of Rome, or else the reprobation of the king's first pretensed matrimony. But if they do obstinately persist in their opinions of the preamble, yet, meseemeth, it should not be refused, if they will be sworn to the very act of succession: so that they will be sworn to maintain the same against all powers and potentates. For hereby shall be a great occasion to satisfy the princess dowager and the lady Mary, which do think they should damn their souls, if they should abandon and relinquish their estates. And not only it should stop the mouths of them, but also of the emperor, and other their friends, if they give as much credence to my lord of Rochester and master More speaking and doing against them, as they hitherto have done, and thought that all other should have done, when they spake and did with them. And peradventure it should be a good quietation to many other within this realm, if such men should say, that the succession comprised within the said act is good and according to God's laws. For then I think there is not one within this realm, that would once reclaim against it.

From a letter from Thomas Cranmer, Archbishop of Canterbury, to Thomas Cromwell, 17 April 1534

### D  Thomas More at his trial [an account by his son-in-law, written in the reign of Queen Mary]

'Forasmuch as, my lord,' quoth he, 'this indictment is grounded upon an act of Parliament directly repugnant to the laws of God and His Holy Church, the supreme government of which, or of any part whereof, may no temporal prince presume by any law to take upon him, as rightfully belonging to the See of Rome, a spiritual pre-eminence by the mouth of Our Saviour himself, personally present upon the earth, only to St Peter and his successors, Bishops of the same See, by special prerogative granted; it is therefore in law, amongst Christian men, insufficient to charge any Christian man.'

And for proof thereof like as (among divers other reasons and authorities) he declared that this realm, being but one member and small part of the Church, might not make a particular law disagreeable with the general law of Christ's universal Catholic Church, no more than the City of London, being but one poor member in respect of the whole realm, might make a law against an act of Parliament to bind the whole realm. . . .

Then was it by the Lord Chancellor [Audley] thereunto answered that, seeing all the bishops, universities, and best learned of this realm had to this act agreed, it was much marvelled that he alone against them all would so stiffly stick thereat, and so vehemently argue there against. To that Sir Thomas More replied, saying:

'If the number of bishops and universities be so material as your lordship seemeth to take it, then see I little cause, my lord, why that thing in my conscience should make any change. For I nothing doubt but that, though not in this realm, yet in Christendom about, of these well-learned bishops and virtuous men that are yet alive, they be not the fewer part that be of my mind therein. But if I should speak of those which already be dead, of whom many be now holy saints in heaven, I am very sure it is the far greater part of them that, all the while they lived, thought in this case that way that I think now. And therefore am I not bound, my lord, to conform my conscience to the council of one realm against the general council of Christendom.'

From William Roper: *The Life of Sir Thomas More*

## E Treason
Be it therefore enacted . . . that if any person or persons, after the first day of February next coming, do maliciously wish, will or desire by words or writing, or by craft imagine, invent, practise or attempt any bodily harm to be done or committed to the King's most royal person, the Queen's or their heir's apparent, or to deprive them or any of them of the dignity, title or name of their royal estates, or slanderously and maliciously publish and pronounce, by express writing or words, that the King our sovereign lord should be heretic, schismatic, tyrant, infidel or usurper of the crown . . . then every such person and persons so offending . . . their aiders, counsellors, consenters and abettors . . . shall be adjudged traitors; and that every such offence . . . shall be reputed, accepted and adjudged high treason. And the offenders therein, and their aiders, consenters, counsellors and abettors, being lawfully convict of any such offence as is aforesaid, shall have and suffer such pains of death and other penalties as is limited and accustomed in cases of high treason.

From An Act Whereby Divers Offences be made High Treason, 1534

## F Local resistance in Exeter in 1536 [written in the reign of Queen Elizabeth]
[The commissioners] . . . beginning first with the priory of St Nicholas, after that they viewed the same they went thence to dinner and commanded [a man] in the time of their absence to pull down the rood loft in the church. In the meanwhile, and before they did return, certain women and wives in the city . . . minding to stop the suppressing of that house, came in all haste to the said church, some with spikes, some with shovels, some with pikes, and some with such tools as they could get and, the church door being fast, they broke it open. And finding there the man pulling down the rood loft they all sought, all the means they could, to take him and hurled stones unto him, in so much that for

his safety he was driven to take to the tower for his refuge. And yet they pursued him so eagerly that he was enforced to leap out at a window and so to save himself, and very hardly he escaped the breaking of his neck, but yet he break one of his ribs. . . . The Mayor . . . came down with his officers, before whose coming they [the women] had made fast the church doors and had bestowed themselves in places meet as they thought to stand to their defences. Notwithstanding, the Mayor broke in upon them and with much ado he apprehended and took them all and sent them to ward.

From the recollection of John Hooker, City Chamberlain of Exeter

**G   The Pilgrimage of Grace [the demands drawn up by the leaders of the Pilgrimage in December 1536]**

 1   The first touching our faith to have the heresies of Luther, Wycliffe, Huss, Melancthon, Oecolampadius, Bucer, Confessio Germaniae, Apologia Melancthonis, the works of Tyndale, of Barnes, of Marshall, of Rastell, Saint German and such other heresies of Anabaptists thereby within this realm to be annulled and destroyed.

 2   The 2nd to have the supreme head of the church touching the care of souls to be restored unto the see of Rome . . .

 3   Item we humbly beseech our most dread sovereign lord that the Lady Mary may be made legitimate . . .

 4   . . . to have the abbeys suppressed to be restored . . .

 5   . . . to have the tenths and first fruits clearly discharged of the same . . .

 6   . . . to have the Friars Observant restored unto their houses again.

 7   . . . to have the heretics, bishops and temporal, and their sect to have condign punishment . . .

 8   . . . to have the Lord Cromwell, the Lord Chancellor, and Sir Richard Rich, knight, to have condign punishment, as the subverters of the good laws of this realm and maintainers of the false sect of those heretics . . .

 9   . . . that the lands in Westmoreland, Cumberland, Kendal, Dent, Sedbergh, Furness and the abbey lands in Mashamshire, Kirkbyshire, Nidderdale, may be by tenant right, and the lord to have at every change two years rent . . . and no more . . .

10   . . . the statutes of handguns and crossbows to be repealed . . .

11   . . . that Doctor Legh and Doctor Layton . . . have condign punishment for their extortions in their time of visitations . . .

12   . . . reformation for the election of knights of [the] shire and burgesses . . .

13   . . . statute for enclosures and intakes to be put in execution . . .

14 ... to be discharged of the quindene [i.e. fifteenth] and taxes now granted by act of Parliament.

15 ... to have the Parliament in a convenient place at Nottingham or York ...

16 ... the statute of the declaration of the crown by will, that the same may be annulled and repealed.

17 ... that it be enacted by act of Parliament that all ... penalties now forfeit during the time of this commotion may be pardoned ...

18 ... the privileges and rights of the Church to be confirmed by act of Parliament ...

19 ... the liberties of the Church to have their old customs ...

20 ... to have the statute that no man shall will his lands to be repealed.

21 ... that the statute of treason for words and such like ... to be in like wise repealed.

22 ... that the common laws may have place as was used in the beginning of your Grace's reign ...

23 ... that no man upon subpoena is from Trent north [to] appear but at York or by attorney, unless it be directed upon pain of allegiance and for like matters concerning the King.

24 ... a remedy against escheators for finding of false offices ...

From the Copy of the Articles to the Lords of the King's Council at our Coming to Pontefract

### H The examination of Ninian Staveley

Ninian Staveley, 34, late of the parish of Masham in Richmondshire, answers that two monks of Jervaulx, Roger Hartylpoole, jun, now fled into Scotland, and John Staynton, lately executed, urged him and Edward Middleton of Masham, likewise fled into Scotland, from Christmas last till Candlemas [i.e. 2 February], to gather a company to destroy the Duke of Norfolk, so that their abbey might stand, and Holy Church be as it was in Henry VII's days; for if Norfolk came into the country their abbey would be put down and they would go a-begging. On Sunday after Candlemas Day they consented, and, with the monks, made bills to set on all church doors of Richmondshire calling all from 16 to 60 to appear at Middleham Moor in harness on Tuesday next.... Staveley and Middleton would have gone no further, but that night at midnight the said two monks came in harness each with a battleaxe in hand to the house of Ninian Staveley, and forced him to rise out of bed, crying that unless he would go forward both he and they should be destroyed. Staveley on this sent his servant to Middleton. 'And the said Staveley and Middleton with their neighbours and friends, to the number of ten, came to the abbey of Jervaulx about noon on the

Tuesday and bade the abbot and all his monks come forth with them. And the abbot said and desired them to be contented to leave his brethren at home, and to take his servants with them, and said further that he and all his brethren would come unto them the next day. And then he gave the company such meat and drink as he had, the abbot quondam of Fountains being there present with him.' The said quondam of Fountains had previously offered Staveley and Middleton, in case of any new insurrection, 20 nobles to restore him to Fountains, saying he was unjustly put out by the visitors. . . . Staveley says that if the said two monks had not called so busily on them they had made no insurrection. . . .

This is the full confession of Staveley and is all true, by the death he shall die which he expects, and knows he deserves.

From the examination of Ninian Staveley, 23 April 1537

## I   Discontent in Cornwall

A friend of mine, a painter, informs me that he was desired by one Carpyssacke, dwelling in St Keverne, to make a banner for the said parish, in which they would have 'the picture of Christ with his wounds abroad and a banner in his hand, Our Lady in the one side holding her breast in her hand, St John a Baptist in the other side, the King's grace and the Queen kneeling, and all the commonalty kneeling, with scripture above their heads making their petition to the picture of Christ that it would please the King's grace that they might have their holidays [i.e. holy days]' as the bearer can declare. . . . Carpyssacke also said he and John Treglosacke had been at Hamell beside Southampton selling their fish, and two men asked them why they rose not when the Northern men did; on which they swore upon a book to help them and had bought 200 jerkins; that they would carry the banner on Pardon Monday and show it among the people. Has made secret inquiry about this proposed stirring and will take care to stop it, for the country is in a marvellous good quiet. Begs Cromwell to move the King that they might hold the day of the head saint of their church and the country would pray for him.

From the summary of a letter from Sir William Godolghan to Thomas Cromwell, 22 April 1537

# Questions

**1** With reference to Source C, explain why Cranmer thought that Fisher and More should be allowed to take the oath. **(3 marks)**

**2** Using your own knowledge, explain the references in Source G to
  **a** the Lady Mary (Item 3)
  **b** Sir Richard Rich (Item 8)
  **c** Doctor Legh and Doctor Layton (Item 11). **(3 marks)**

**3** How reliable do you think Source H is as evidence of the Pilgrimage of Grace? **(5 marks)**

**4** To what extent do these sources indicate that opposition to Henry VIII was primarily for religious reasons? **(7 marks)**

**5** Using the sources and your own knowledge, account for the limited success of opposition to Henry VIII. **(12 marks)**

# 5 EDWARD VI: THE PROTESTANT REFORMATION

Under Edward VI England became an officially Protestant country. For example, the dissolution of the chantries, foundations dedicated to praying for the dead, marked the rejection of the Catholic doctrine of Purgatory. Cranmer's two Prayer Books, for all their debts to past liturgies, were the products of a Protestant establishment. The impact on the average person's religious practice was much greater than in Henry's reign. Now, when the parishioners went to church, they heard the service in English, presided over by a minister who might be married and would no longer be wearing the full vestments of Catholicism, in a building that had been stripped of most of its devotional lights and images [A-D, K]. Here was change indeed – how did people react to it? Not everyone was as extreme as those of the West Country, who in 1549 rose in armed rebellion against the changes, demanding a return to the old Latin services and traditional religious practices [L]. However, there must have been many who resented what was happening, especially when they saw church furnishings or plate that they or their families had paid for, being ripped out or taken off to the royal treasury.

Protestants at the time were well aware of the difficulties they faced and their letters comment on the shortage of able and committed preachers who could be sent out to win the people over to the new ways. In London and some other centres they felt strong, but this was not the case throughout the country. At the same time the Protestants had their own internal disputes over such problems as the role of bishops, the wearing of vestments and the nature of the Eucharist [C, G].

If there was no popular demand for the changes, where did the initiative come from? On the death of Henry VIII the reforming faction at court had managed to gain the advantage and dominate the new King's council under the Lord Protector, the Duke of Somerset. It is difficult to tell the extent to which either he or the Duke of Northumberland, who effectively succeeded to his position in 1550, was sincerely committed to reform or simply saw it as a means of enriching themselves and the crown from the spoils of the Church. They had also to take into account the feelings of their King, who even at his young age had shown himself to be an ardent supporter of reform. How far did they, and others, conform to Protestantism in anticipation of Edward's coming of age when continued favour and influence would surely depend on the appropriate religious loyalty? How active, despite his youth, was Edward himself in the religious policy of his reign?

## A  Reformation from above

After our right hearty commendations to your good lordship, where now of late, in the king's majesty's visitation, among other godly injunctions ... one was set forth for the taking down all such images as had at any time been abused with pilgrimages, offerings, or censings. Albeit, that this said injunction hath in many parts of the realm been well and quietly obeyed and executed, yet in many other places much strife and contention hath arisen ... some men being so superstitious, or rather wilful, as they would ... retain all such images ... and in some places also, the images which ... were taken down, be now restored. ...

Considering therefore, that almost in no places of the realm is any sure quietness, but where all images be wholly taken away ... you shall not only give order that all the images remaining in any church or chapel within your diocese be removed and taken away, but also by your letters signify unto the rest of the bishops within your province, this his highness' pleasure, for the like order to be given by them ...

An Order of the Council for the Removing of Images, 21 February 1547

## B  The prohibition of books and images

Where the king's most excellent majesty hath of late set forth and established by authority of parliament an uniform, quiet, and godly order for common and open prayer, in a book entitled The Book of Common Prayer much more conformable unto his loving subjects than other diversity of service as heretofore of long time hath been used ... Be it therefore enacted ... that all ... other books or writings whatsoever heretofore used for service of the church, written or printed in the English or the Latin tongue, other than such as are or shall be set forth by the king's majesty, shall be by authority of this present act clearly and utterly abolished, extinguished, and forbidden for ever to be used or kept in this realm ...

II And be it further enacted ... that if any person or persons ... that now have or hereafter shall have in his, her, or their custody any the books or writings of the sort aforesaid, or any images of stone, timber, alabaster, or earth, graven, carved, or painted, which heretofore have been taken out of any church or chapel, or yet stand in any church or chapel, and do not before the last day of June next ensuing deface and destroy ... the same images ... and deliver ... all and every the same books ... either to be openly burnt or otherways defaced and destroyed shall ... forfeit and lose to the king our sovereign lord for the first offence twenty shillings, and for the second offence ... four pounds, and for the third offence shall suffer imprisonment at the king's will.

From An Act for the abolishing and putting away of divers books and images, 1550

### C   A bishop's Injunctions

First, That there be no reading of such injunctions as extolleth and setteth forth the popish mass, candles, images, chantries ...

Item, That no minister do counterfeit the popish mass ... that the minister, in the time of the holy communion, do use only the ceremonies and gestures appointed by the Book of Common Prayer, and none other, so that there do not appear in them any counterfeiting of the popish mass ...

Item, Whereas in divers places some use the Lord's board after the form of a table, and some of an altar, whereby dissension is perceived to arise among the unlearned; therefore wishing a godly unity to be observed in all our diocese, and for that the form of a table may more move and turn the simple from the old superstitious opinions of the popish mass and to the right use of the Lord's Supper, we exhort the curates, churchwardens and questmen here present, to erect and set up the Lord's board, after the form of an honest table, decently covered, in such place of the quire or chancel as shall be thought most meet by their discretion and agreement, so that the ministers, with the communicants, may have their place separated from the rest of the people; and to take down and abolish all other by-altars and tables.

From Nicholas Ridley's Injunctions to his diocese of London, 1550

### D   A London chronicle

... the 5th day after in September [1547] began the king's visitation at Paul's, and all the images pulled down; and the 9th day of the same month the said visitation was at St Bride's, and after that in divers other parish churches; and so all images pulled down through all England at that time, and all churches new white-limed, with the commandments written on the walls ...

Item at this same time was pulled up all the tombs, great stones, all the altars, with the stalls and walls of the choir and altars in the church that was some time the Grey Friars, and sold, and the choir made smaller ...

Item the 17th day of [November] at night was pulled down the rood in Paul's, with Mary and John, with all the images in the church ... at that same time was pulled down through all the king's dominion in every church all roods with all images, and every preacher preached in their sermons against all images ...

Item this year [1548] was all the chantries put down ...

Item the 7th day of July after there was a priest that came out of Cornwall drawn from the Tower of London unto Smithfield and there was hanged and beheaded and quartered for slaying of one Boddy, that was the king's commissioner in that country for suppressing chantries ...

Item the 20th day of June [1549] the which was Corpus Christi day, and as that day in divers places in London was kept holy day, and many kept none, but did work openly, and in some churches service and some none, such was the division ...

Item the 4th day of September [1552] was upon a Sunday, and then the choir of St Paul's had a commandment from the dean from Cambridge at the bishop of Canterbury's visitation that he should leave the playing of organs at the divine service and so left it ...

Item the 25th day of October was the plucking down of all the altars and chapels in Paul's church, with all the tombs, at the commandment of the bishop then being Nicholas Ridley, and all the goodly stonework that stood behind the high altar, and the place for the priest, deacon and sub-deacon; and would have pulled down John of Gaunt's tomb but there was a commandment to the contrary from the Council, and so it was all made plain as it appears.

From the Chronicle of the Grey Friars of London, a contemporary account

**E**  **The Reformation in the parishes: a fifteenth century reredos at St Cuthbert's Church, Wells, Somerset [Statues were removed from the niches, carving hacked away and the whole design plastered over. It was uncovered in 1848]**

**F  Miscellaneous expenses and receipts**

**1548**  **Payments**

Item, paid for the hewing down of the seats of the images in the church and whiteliming the church          xvd

**1548–9**  **Receipts**

... for a lamp and censer ...                              iiijs
... for a copper cross                                    ijs
... for a holy water pot of lead and certain organ
pipes ...                                                 ijs   xd
... for the case of the organs                               viijd
... for the coffer of the organs                          ijs

**Payments**

| | |
|---|---|
| . . . for writing of ij inventories of the church goods to the king's commissioners | viijd |
| . . . for ij forms for the communion to be received at | iiijs |
| . . . for writing of scriptures and painting the church | xiijs iiijd |
| . . . for taking down of the altars and paving where the said altars stood | iijs iiijd |

**1552–3  Receipts**

| | |
|---|---|
| . . . for the rood loft | xvs  ijd |

**Payments**

| | |
|---|---|
| . . . for taking down of the rood loft to Richard Mitte for ij days work | xxs |

From the Churchwardens' Accounts of St Michael's in Bedwardine, Worcester

## G  A comment on the communion table

First they placed it aloft, where the high altar stood. Then down it must come. . . . In some places beneath the steps, in the quire, covering it about with a curtain for fear of bugs. Within a while after, it skipped out of the quire into the body of the church. And in some places neither in the quire nor yet in the body of the church but between both. And some, because they would hit it right, pulled down the rood-loft, making such a confusion that neither was there a quire nor body of the church, but making it like Westminster Hall.

From Miles Hogarde: *The Displaying of the Protestants and sundry their practices with a description of divers their abuses of late frequented within their malignant church* (1556)

## H  A request to the continental reformers

We are anxious to set forth in our churches the true doctrine of God, and have no desire to be shifting and unstable, or to deal in ambiguities. . . . To carry out this great work we have thought it necessary to have the assistance of learned men, who after exchanging opinions with us, may do away with doctrinal controversies, and build up a complete system of true doctrine. We have, therefore, invited both yourself and some other scholars, and as they have come over to us quite willingly, so that we scarcely have to regret the absence of any of them, save yourself and Melancthon we earnestly beg for you both to come yourself and bring Melancthon with you if you possibly can. I am now sending a third letter to Melancthon begging him to come to us; and if your exhortations are added to my letter I am sure he will be persuaded to accept an invitation repeated so many times.

Thomas Cranmer to John a Lasco, 4 July 1548

## I Links with the continental reformers

If I am now able to effect anything, and my slender powers are of any benefit to the church of Christ, I confess . . . that I owe it to yourself and my masters and brethren at Zurich. . . . Moreover, if you have any thing which you purpose soon to send to the press, you should dedicate it to our most excellent sovereign, king Edward VI. . . . If you will comply with my wishes in this respect, you will advance the glory of God in no small degree.

John Hooper to Henry Bullinger, 27 December 1549

## J The influence of the continental reformers on the King

Great evil is impending over the Church of England, and I know that all worthy and godly persons are exceedingly distressed. This evil, however, may easily be either removed or mitigated by your authority, and that of your church, if you will write to the king. Hooper is striving to effect an entire purification of the church from the very foundation. Other bishops . . . contend with all their might to have him entangled in the same superstitious ceremonies with themselves. . . . The controversy now rests with the king to determine, who if he be clearly instructed by you as to the judgement that must be formed of it according to God's word, I have no doubt but that it will be of great advantage to religion.

John Burcher to Henry Bullinger, 28 December 1550

## K A Protestant artist depicts Edward's reign [from the 1570 edition of John Foxe's *Acts and Monuments*]

### L   Resistance

Item we will have the mass in Latin, as was before, and celebrated by the priest without any man or woman communicating with him.

. . . we will have holy bread and holy water made every Sunday, palms and ashes at the times accustomed, images to be set up again in every church, and all other ancient old ceremonies used heretofore, by our mother the holy Church.

. . . we will not receive the new service because it is but like a Christmas game, but we will have our old service of matins, mass, evensong and procession in Latin not in English, as it was before. And so we Cornish men (whereof certain of us understand no English) utterly refuse this new English.

. . . we will have every preacher in his sermon, and every priest at his mass, pray specially by name for the souls in Purgatory, as our forefathers did.

. . . we will have the whole Bible and all books of scripture in English to be called in again, for we be informed that otherwise the clergy shall not of long time confound the heretics.

From the demands of the Western Rebels, 1549

### M   The end of the reign

A few days before his death the king made a will at the instigation of Northumberland, by which he disinherited both his sisters, and appointed the lady Frances, wife of the Duke of Suffolk, to be his heir. She declined it and the kingdom was made over to her daughter Jane. . . . Jane is brought down to take possession of the Tower, and on the same day is proclaimed queen at London, and in the same week in many parts of the kingdom. Mary, who had most faithful councillors, by their advice went, as though defenceless, into Norfolk, where she is received and hailed as queen with general applause. . . . Almost the entire nation rise to her assistance; first of all the people of Norfolk and Suffolk, and then those of Oxfordshire, Buckinghamshire, Berkshire and Essex. . . . After some days Mary made her entry with great triumph into the city, to take possession of the Tower . . .

The queen, partly with a view of ascertaining the popular feeling, and partly for the encouragement of her partisans, sets forth a proclamation, in which she declares her adherence to and protection and support of popery, and exhorts all persons to conform to it; but nevertheless at that time she would compel no one to embrace it.

The papists, who had been always longing for this most wished for day, dig out as it were from their graves their vestments, chalices, and portasses, and begin mass with all speed. In these things our Oxford folk lead the van; and respecting them I must tell you a little farther. At the proclamation of Jane they displayed nothing but grief. At the proclamation of Mary, even before she was proclaimed at London, and when the event was still doubtful, they gave such demonstrations of joy, as to spare nothing. They first of all made so much noise all the day long with clapping their hands, that it seems still to linger in my ears; they then, even the poorest of them, made voluntary subscriptions, and mutually exhorted each other to maintain the cause of Mary; lastly, at night they had a public festival, and threatened flames, hanging, the gallows and drowning to all the gospellers.

The Protestant reformer Julius Terentianus to John ab Ulmis, November 1553

## Questions

**1** How reliable is Source D as evidence of the real progress of the Protestant Reformation in England during Edward VI's reign?

**(6 marks)**

**2** Compare and explain the attitudes to the positioning of the communion table in Sources C and G. **(7 marks)**

**3** With reference to Sources A to G, and using your own knowledge, assess the impact of the Reformation in Edward's reign on the physical appearance of the churches. **(8 marks)**

**4 a** To what extent do Sources H, I and J demonstrate the relationship between the Reformation in England and the Reformation in Europe? **(5 marks)**

**b** What are the advantages and disadvantages of using letters like those in Sources H, I and J as evidence about the Reformation?

**(5 marks)**

**5** Comment on the value of Source K as evidence for the events of Edward VI's reign. **(6 marks)**

**6** 'Things are for the most part carried on by means of ordinances, which the people obey very grudgingly' (Martin Bucer, 1550). To what extent do these sources support this statement? **(10 marks)**

# 6 MARY I: THE CATHOLIC REFORMATION

When Mary came to the throne in 1553 her religious views were already well known. She had been able to retain the Latin mass in her own household during the first part of Edward's reign and although that privilege was withdrawn in about 1550 she continued in her refusal to conform to the new Protestantism. When Edward died, the Duke of Northumberland failed in his attempt to keep her from the throne and her accession was swiftly followed by the restoration of Catholic practices.

New bishops were appointed or old ones restored – for example Gardiner to Winchester [A] and Bonner to London – and, under the leadership of Cardinal Reginald Pole, previously in exile and now Archbishop of Canterbury, they set about the task of restoring Catholic doctrine and practices in the English Church [B-D, J] What were the problems they faced? How deeply rooted was Protestantism at this date and what kind of resistance could be expected from its adherents [I]? Edward's reign had resulted in considerable physical alteration in the churches; what resources of time and money were going to be needed to repair the damage? After all, it takes relatively little skill or time to pull down and burn a rood screen or its statues, but replacing them is a different matter. Full reconciliation with Rome came late in 1554 when Cardinal Pole lifted the sentence of excommunication that had been laid on England and Parliament repealed all the anti-papal legislation that had been passed in the previous two reigns.

It is difficult to predict how successful these steps would have been in the long run, if Mary had lived to pursue her policies, but one factor that needs to be considered in attempting such a judgement is the burning of the Protestants [E-F]. Were these counter-productive, encouraging rather than weakening the Protestant cause? How did the English people react to them generally? Similar events took place in other countries; was England so different that it was unlikely to be reconciled to such a large number of burnings in so short a time? Certainly they became the focus of criticism of Mary's reign for future generations but does that reflect the contemporary view [K]?

The same question might be asked of Mary's marriage to Philip of Spain. It was not supported by all her advisers and that it took place was very much the result of her own insistence, but to what extent was it genuinely unpopular [G-H]? True, it could be used by Sir Thomas Wyatt and others in raising rebellion against the Queen but political ambition,

Protestantism and economic problems may have contributed as much to their support. Was it the later association of the Spanish marriage with the harsh treatment of Protestants that led later generations to project their own attitudes back to the reign of Queen Mary?

## A    A call to action from Stephen Gardiner

On Sunday the 11th day of February [1554], the bishop of Winchester preached in the chapel before the queen, beginning at 3 of the clock with *exhortemur*, the sixth chapter of the second epistle to the Corinthians; wherein he treated first, that man had free will; next, that Lent was necessarily appointed by the Church for christian men; thirdly, that works were a mean or way to Heaven, and thereby the sooner we might obtain the fruition of our redemption by Christ; fourthly, that the preachers for the seven years last past, by dividing of words, and other their own additions, had brought in many errors detestable unto the Church of Christ; fifthly, and lastly, he asked a boon of the queen's highness that like as she had before time extended her mercy, particularly and privately, so through her lenity and gentleness much conspiracy and open rebellion was grown . . . which he brought then in for the purpose that she would now be merciful to the body of the commonwealth, and conservation thereof, which could not be unless the rotten and hurtful members thereof were cut off and consumed. And thus he ended soon after; whereby all the audience did gather there should shortly follow sharp and cruel execution. Note, he prayed for King Edward VI in his sermon, and for the souls departed.

From *The Chronicle of Queen Jane* . . . written by a resident in the Tower of London, a contemporary account (1554)

## B    An official statement of policy

First Decree

On the thanks that should be given to God for the return of this kingdom to the unity of the Church by the daily celebration of mass and the annual memorial of the same.

Second Decree

On the constitutions, dogmas, and books which should be accepted or rejected and the teaching of canon law.

Third Decree

On the residence of bishops and other lower orders of clergy . . .

Fourth Decree

That bishops and others who have a cure of souls should preach to the people and parish priests should teach children the basic elements of the faith.

Fifth Decree
    On the life and reputation of the clergy.

Sixth Decree
    On the bestowal of ecclesiastical orders and the examination of candidates for ordination.

Seventh Decree
    On the provision of benefices in the church . . .

Ninth Decree
    On simony . . .

Eleventh Decree
    That in the cathedrals a certain number of boys should be educated, from which, as if from a seed-bed, it will be possible to raise up those who are worthy of a career in the Church . . .

From the decrees of Cardinal Pole's Westminster synod, 1555

## C   Restoring Catholicism: Cardinal Pole's Injunctions

III Item, that all parsons, vicars and curates shall every holiday, when there is a sermon, at the sermon time plainly recite and diligently teach the Pater Noster, the Ave Maria, the Crede and the Ten Commandments, in English; exhorting their parishioners to teach the same likewise to their young children at home . . .

XVI Item that the churchwardens of every parish shall see provided and bought at the parish charge all these things hereafter following, where any of the same are at this present lacking; that is to wit, a decent tabernacle set in the midst of the high altar, to preserve the most blessed sacrament under lock and key, after the example of the tabernacle in the cathedral church at Gloucester, every parish as nigh as their ability shall extend unto, with a taper or lamp burning before the same; a decent rood of five foot in length at the least, with Mary and John, and the patron or head saint of the church, proportionate to the same, not painted upon cloth or boards, but cut out in timber or stone; a homily book for the time commanded, as at this present, a book lately set forth entitled 'A Necessary Doctrine': and generally all other things, which after the custom of the place, and the greatness of the parishioners, are bound to find and maintain; and all these things to be provided with all convenient speed upon their peril.

*From The Injunctions given in the visitation of the most reverend father in God, the Lord Cardinal Pole's grace, legate de latere, by his sub-delegate James, by the permission of God bishop of Gloucester, throughout his diocese of Gloucester*

### D   A petition to Cardinal Pole

Item, where our church is greatly defaced, our quire pulled down, our bells and organs be broken, our altars and chapels are by Hooper [Bishop of Worcester under Edward VI] violated and overthrown; our humble desire is to your grace to bestow for a time in reparations of the premises such money as by the order of our statutes we are bounden yearly to spend in the reparation of highways, at the oversight and approbation of my lord bishop . . .

Finally when there be 40 scholars in the free school founded of our alms and beside them 10 choristers to serve the choir, we would wish it might please your grace to permit us to have 14 in the choir and but 36 in the grammar school, for so always as the choristers' breasts do change we might remove them to the grammar school there to continue until they be priests and able to serve the choir again in the singing of the gospel and epistle and in other offices in the church. And also we desire to have it ordained that none with us be admitted but poor men's children only that mind to be priests, according to our statutes.

From a petition of the Dean and Chapter of Worcester Cathedral to Cardinal Pole, early 1558

### E   The Protestant martyrs

#### (i) Unnamed lady to Bonner, bishop of London under Mary I
The blood of the martyrs is the seed of the gospel; when one is put to death a thousand doth rise for him.

#### (ii) From John Ponet: *A Short Treatise of Politik Power* (1556)
. . . to be slaughtered, spoken evil of, whipped, scourged, spoiled of their goods, killed of the worldly princes and tyrants, rather than they would disobey God and forsake Christ; this can neither papists nor Turks, Jews nor Gentiles, nor none other do, but only the Elect of God.

#### (iii) From John Christopherson: *An exhortation to all menne to take hede and beware of rebellion* (1554)
And if they be troubled . . . and peradventure shut up in prison, let them not glory in their fetters as though they were apostles, and write letters of comfort one to another in an apostle's style . . . nor let them not exhort one another to stick fast in their fond opinions.

### F   The burnings

Sire: The people of this town of London are murmuring about the cruel enforcement of the recent acts of Parliament on heresy which has now begun, as shown publicly when a certain Rogers was burnt yesterday. Some of the onlookers wept, others prayed God to give them strength, perseverance, and patience to bear the pain and not to recant, others gathered the ashes and bones and wrapped them up in paper to preserve them, yet others threatening the bishops. The haste with which the bishops have proceeded in this matter may well cause a revolt. Although it may seem necessary to apply exemplary punishment during your Majesty's presence here and under your authority, and to do so before winter is over to intimidate others, I do not think it well that your Majesty should allow further executions to take place unless the reasons are overwhelmingly strong and the offences committed have been so scandalous as to render this course justifiable in the eyes of the people. . . . Otherwise, I foresee that the people may be indisposed, although hitherto they have proved peaceable enough and well-disposed towards your Majesty. If this were to happen, which God forbid, and if the people got the upper hand, not only would the cause of religion be again menaced, but the persons of your Majesty and the Queen might be in peril. . . . Your Majesty might inform the bishops that there are other means of chastising the obstinate, at this early stage: such as secret executions, banishment and imprisonment . . .

From a letter from Simon Renard, the Spanish ambassador, to Philip II, 5 February 1555

## G   The succession
(i) This year [1554], the 27th day of November did the parliament sit at the court at Whitehall in the chamber of presence, where the queen sat highest, richly apparelled, and her belly laid out, that all men might see that she was with child. At this parliament they said labour was made to have the king crowned, and some thought that the queen for that cause did lay out her belly the more. On the right hand of the queen sat the king; and on the other hand of him the cardinal, with his cap on his head: who made an oration, that Pope Julius III had sent them his benediction and blessing, upon their reconciliation again.

From a contemporary account, quoted in J.G. Nichols: *Narratives of the Days of the Reformation* (1859)

(ii) The 30th day of April 1555 . . . tidings came to London that the Queen's grace was delivered of a prince, and so there was great ringing through London, and divers places *Te Deum Laudamus* sung: and the morrow after it was turned otherwise to the pleasure of God. But it shall be when it please God, for I trust God that he will remember his true servants that put their trust in him, when that they call on him.

From the diary of Henry Machyn, a contemporary account (1555)

### H   A divided parish [the writer was a Protestant minister in Edward VI's reign who fled abroad during the reign of Queen Mary]

Queen Mary was proclaimed queen, in whose time the Church of Christ did flourish and was tried by the death of many virtuous, learned, and godly martyrs of Christ Jesus. Queen Mary . . . did set forth a proclamation, which came to my hands, which did declare what religion she did profess in her youth, that she did continue in the same, and that she minded to end her life in the same religion: willing all her loving subjects to embrace the same. This proclamation did so encourage the papists that they, forgetting their duty and obedience to God, and to declare their obedience unto their queen, would have the mass and other superstitious ceremonies in post haste . . . and so did old Thomas Whyght, John Notheral, and others, build up an altar in the church, and had procured a fit chaplain, a French priest, one Sir Brysse, to say their mass; but their altar was pulled down, and Sir Brysse was fain to hide his head, and the papists to build them an altar in old Master Whyght's house, John Craddock his man being clerk to ring the bell, and to help the priest to mass, until he was threatened that if he did use to put his hand out of the window to ring the bell, that a hand-gun should make him to smart, that he should not pull in his hand again with ease.

From the *Autobiography of Thomas Hancock*

### I   A Yorkshireman's view [written early in the reign of Queen Elizabeth by a Yorkshire clergyman]

And so the said Queen Mary was proclaimed at York on the 21st day of July and at Pontefract, Doncaster, Rotherham and many other market towns on the 22nd July . . . she to be right inheritor and Queen of England and Ireland as is above said, whereat the whole commonalty in all places in the north parts greatly rejoiced, making great fires, drinking wine and ale, praising God. But all such as were of heretical opinions, with bishops and priests having wives, did nothing rejoice, but began to be ashamed of themselves, for the common people would point them with fingers in places where they saw them. . . .

In the meantime in many places of the realm priests was commanded by lords and knights catholic to say mass in Latin with consecration and elevation of the body and blood of Christ under form of bread and wine with a decent order as hath been used before time, but such as was of heretical opinions might not away therewith but spake evil thereof, for as then there was no act, statute, proclamation or commandment set forth for the same; therefore many one durst not be bold to celebrate in Latin, though their hearts were wholly inclined that way . . .

Thus through the grace of the Holy Ghost, the strait of the holy Church something began to amend and to arise from the old heresies before used in this realm, for the holy mass in Latin was put down totally from the feast of Pentecost anno domini 1549 unto the beginning of August anno domini 1553, but then in many places of Yorkshire priests unmarried was very glad to celebrate and say mass in Latin with matins and evensong thereto, according for very fervent zeal and love that they had unto God and his laws. And so in the beginning of September there was very few parish churches in Yorkshire but mass was sung or said in Latin on the first Sunday of the said month or at furthest on the feast day of the Nativity of Our Blessed Lady [8 Sep].

Holy bread and holy water was given, altars was re-edified, pictures or images set up, the cross with the crucifix thereon ready to be borne in procession, and with the same went procession. And in conclusion all the English service of late used in the church of God was voluntarily laid away and the Latin taken up again . . . and yet all this came to pass without compulsion of any act, statute, proclamation or law. . . . But such as was of heretical opinions spake evil thereof . . .

And so to proceed further with the matter, in the month of October then next following was also a great parliament held at Westminster wherein all such acts was utterly abolished and fordone as had been made afore time against the Pope of Rome . . . and so with speed it was published and proclaimed in every shire within this realm. . . . Then began holy Church to rejoice in God, singing both with heart and tongue . . . but heretical persons (as there was many) rejoiced nothing thereat. Hoo, it was joy to hear and see how these carnal priests (which had led their lives in fornication with their whores and harlots) did lour and look down, when they were commanded to leave and foresake the concubines and harlots and to do open penance according to the canon law, which then took effect.

From the *Narrative of Robert Parkyn*

## J   An Italian's view
It is indubitable that externally and in appearance the catholic religion seems day by day to increase and take root, through the queen's authority and the assiduity of the legate, for the monasteries are being built, and within this short period (three years not yet having elapsed since the reducement of the realm) when I left England seven were completed; persons are seen to enter them, the churches are frequented, the images replaced, and all the ancient catholic rites and ceremonies performed as they used to be, the heretical being suppressed. These things are done either from fear or to deceive, some persons, by appearing catholics, wishing to ingratiate themselves with the queen. . . . But with the exception of a few most pious catholics . . . none of whom however is under thirty-five years of age, all the rest

make this show of recantation ... and on the first opportunity would be more than ever ready and determined to return to the unrestrained life previously led by them. ...

With regard however to religion, in general, your Serenity may rest assured that the example and authority of their sovereign can do anything with them. ... On these grounds, many people who are more in their confidence are of the opinion that could they feel sure of not being molested about the church property held by them, when a little more accustomed to the present religion, they would adapt themselves even to that, but they are still afraid of being one day or another compelled to give back all or part of it ...

From the report of the Venetian ambassador to the Doge and Senate, May 1557

## Questions

1 Using your own knowledge, comment on Gardiner's choice of the first three topics in the sermon in Source A. **(5 marks)**

2 What practical problems in the restoration of Catholicism are indicated in Sources C and D? **(4 marks)**

3 Use the evidence of Sources A, E(i)-(iii) and F to assess Mary's wisdom in pursuing such a harsh policy against the Protestants. **(6 marks)**

4 Comment on the significance of the extracts in Sources G(i) and G(ii) **(5 marks)**

5 Could Source H be used more appropriately to support an argument in favour of the strength of Catholic feeling or in favour of the strength of Protestant feeling? Explain your answer. **(6 marks)**

6 a To what extent do Sources I and J differ in the impressions they give of religious opinion in England during Mary's reign? **(4 marks)**
  b How can you explain these differences? **(4 marks)**
  c Compare the advantages and disadvantages of Source I and Source J as evidence of religious opinion at this time. **(5 marks)**

7 To what extent do these sources support the view that Mary's religious policy was essentially negative? **(10 marks)**

# 7 THOMAS CRANMER

Thomas Cranmer was a central figure in the English Reformation. In one way or another he has a link with almost every chapter in this book. He was a Cambridge scholar until 1529 when some comments he made on how the King might set about getting his annulment brought him to Henry's notice and the beginning of his public career. In 1533 he became Archbishop of Canterbury [A], chosen by Henry [C] but appointed and consecrated with the approval of the Pope, and he remained the King's loyal servant until the end of the reign. Cranmer had had Protestant leanings for many years but it was only in the reign of Edward that he could put his ideas fully into effect [D], supported by the young King himself and his guardians, Somerset and Northumberland. After the death of Edward, he was arrested for treason since he had cooperated in the plot to put Lady Jane Grey on the throne, then condemned as a heretic and burned at the stake in 1556 [J, K].

Cranmer's career demonstrates the influence one individual can have. Even before his appointment as archbishop, while on an embassy for Henry, he had made close contact with German Protestants and married the niece of a Lutheran minister in Germany. Despite this he always enjoyed a particularly close relationship with Henry and this meant that the reforming cause was never totally abandoned during that King's reign. Later he produced the Book of Common Prayer [E] which, with minor alterations, remained the prayer book of the Anglican Church for more than four hundred years, and the Forty-Two Articles of Religion that he published at the very end of Edward VI's reign became the basis for the Thirty-Nine Articles that were accepted as the summary of Anglican doctrine in the reign of Elizabeth.

He has not always enjoyed a high reputation even among Protestants. Could he have been more forthright in his Protestantism under Henry VIII and did he not dither too much when Mary came to the throne, first signing a recantation of his Protestant beliefs and only denying that recantation when he realised he had not escaped execution [I]? A major Catholic criticism was that of hypocrisy. Before his consecration as archbishop he had publicly declared that no oath of loyalty to the Pope could bind him to act against the King or prevent his taking part in any reformation of the English church that he should think necessary. How, his opponents asked, could that be reconciled to his oath as archbishop?

How valid are these criticisms of Cranmer? Was he simply an

ambitious prelate of Protestant rather than Catholic persuasion? Was he a sincere but possibly weak reformer? How far do such judgements take into account the situation in which he found himself, the people with whom he had to deal and the responsibility he bore as Archbishop of Canterbury?

A  **A portrait of Thomas Cranmer by Gerlach Flicke, 1546 [Cranmer holds a copy of Paul's Epistles, the larger bound book is St Augustine's *On Faith and Works*, and the letter is addressed 'To the most Rev. Father in God & my singular good lord, my Lord the Archbishop of Canterbury, his grace, be this . . .']**

**B   A portrait of Archbishop William Warham by Hans Holbein, 1527**

## C   Henry's Archbishop

You were born in a happy hour I suppose for, do or say what you will,
the king will always well take it at your hands. And I must needs confess
that in some things I have complained of you unto his majesty, but all in
vain for he will never give credit against you, whatsoever is laid to your
charge; but let me or any other of the council be complained of, his
grace will most seriously chide and fall out with us. And therefore you
are most happy, if you can keep you in this estate.

Thomas Cromwell to Cranmer, 1539

## D   Cranmer the Reformer . . .
### (i) . . . is luke-warm

As to [the Archbishop of] Canterbury, he conducts himself in such a
way, I know not how, as that the people do not think much of him, and
the nobility regard him as luke-warm. In other respects he is a kind and
good-natured man.

Bartholomew Traheran to Henry Bullinger, 1 August 1548

### (ii) . . . has fallen into a slumber

But, to tell you all in a few words, although your letter . . . afforded pleasure to everyone, and to the archbishop himself a full gratifying exhortation to his duty; yet I would have you know this for certain, that this Thomas has fallen into so heavy a slumber, that we entertain but a very cold hope that he will be aroused even by your most learned letter. For he has lately published a Catechism, in which he has not only approved that foul and sacrilegious transubstantiation of the papists in the holy supper of our Saviour, but all the dreams of Luther seem to him sufficiently well-grounded, perspicuous and lucid.

John ab Ulmis to Henry Bullinger, 18 August 1548

### (iii) . . . is firm and learned

On the 14 December . . . a disputation was held at London concerning the eucharist. . . . The argument was sharply contested by the bishops. The Archbishop of Canterbury, contrary to general expectation, most openly, firmly and learnedly maintained your opinion upon this subject. . . . Next followed the bishop of Rochester, Ridley, who handles the subject . . . as to stop the mouth of that most zealous papist, the bishop of Worcester. The truth never obtained a more brilliant victory among us.

Bartholomew Traheran to Henry Bullinger, 31 December 1548

### E   Cranmer's Prayer Book – the Communion Service

| 1549 Edition | 1552 Edition |
|---|---|
| . . . the Priest . . . shall put upon him . . . a white alb plain, with a vestment or Cope . . . | . . . the minister . . . shall use neither alb, vestment nor cope . . . he shall have and wear a surplice only . . . |
| The Priest standing humbly afore the middle of the Altar . . . | And the Priest standing at the north side of the Table . . . |
| And when he delivereth the Sacrament of the body of Christ, he shall say to everyone these words | And when he delivereth the bread, he shall say |
| The body of our Lord Jesus Christ which was given for thee, preserve thy body and soul unto everlasting life. | Take and eat this, in remembrance that Christ died for thee, and feed on him in thy heart by faith, with thanksgiving. |

| | |
|---|---|
| And the Minister delivering the Sacrament of the blood . . . shall say | And the Minister that delivereth the cup, shall say |
| The blood of our Lord Jesus Christ which was shed for thee, preserve thy body and soul unto everlasting life . . . | Drink this in remembrance that Christ's blood was shed for thee and be thankful . . . |
| For avoiding of all matters and occasion of dissension, it is meet that the bread prepared for the Communion be made . . . unleavened and round, as it was afore . . . | And to take away the superstition . . . it shall suffice that the bread be such as is usual to be eaten at Table . . . and if any of the bread or wine remain, the Curate shall have it to his own use . . . |

From the *Book of Common Prayer*, 1549 and 1552

## F   A lenient adversary [written by Cranmer's secretary]

Again, one thing he commonly used wherein many did discommend him, which was this: he always bare a good face and countenance unto the papists, and would both in word and deed do very much for them, pardoning their offences; and on the other side, somewhat over severe against the protestants; which being perceived not to be done but upon some purpose, on a time a friend of his declared unto him that he therein did very much harm, encouraging thereby the papists, and also thereby in discouraging the protestants. Whereunto he made this answer and said, 'What will ye have a man do to him that is not yet come to the knowledge of the truth of the gospel, nor peradventure yet called, and whose vocation is to me uncertain? Shall we perhaps, in his journey coming towards us, by severity and cruel behaviour overthrow him, and as it were in his voyage stop him? I take not this the way to allure men to embrace the doctrine of the gospel. And if it be a true rule of our Saviour Christ to do good for evil, then let such as are not yet come to favour our religion learn to follow the doctrine of the gospel by our example, in using them friendly and charitably. On the other side, such as have tasted of sincere religion, and as it were taken hold of the gospel, and seem in words to maintain the true doctrine thereof, and then by the evil example of their lives most perniciously become stumbling blocks unto such as are weak, and not at all as yet entered into this voyage, what would you have me do with them? bear with them and wink at their faults, and so willingly suffer the gospel (by their outrageous doings) to be trodden under our feet?' . . . And thus . . . he answered mine eldest brother, who was earnest with him for the amendment of this his quality. Mr Isaac, yet living, is a witness of the matter.

From Ralph Morice: *Anecdotes and Character of Archbishop Cranmer* (*c.*1565)

### G Edward Underhill chides Cranmer

Thus passed I forth the time at Limehouse. . . . I had there fierce enemies, specially the vicar of Stepney, abbot quondam of Tower Hill, whom I apprehended in King Edward's time and carried him unto Croydon to Cranmer, [Arch]bishop of Canterbury; for that he disturbed preachers in his church, causing the bells to be rung when they were at the sermon, and sometimes begin to sing in the choir before the sermon were half done, and sometimes challenge the preacher in the pulpit . . . [Cranmer] was too full of lenity: a little he rebuked him and bade him do no more so. 'My lord,' said I, 'methinks you are too gentle unto so stout a papist.' 'Well,' said he, 'we have no law to punish them by.' 'We have, my lord,' said I, 'if I had your authority I would be so bold as to unvicar him, or administer some sharp punishment unto him and such other. If it ever come to their turn, they will show you no such favour.' 'Well,' said he, 'if God so provide, we must abide it.' 'Surely,' said I, 'God will never give you thanks for this, but rather take the sword from such as will not use it upon his enemies.' And thus we departed.

From the *Autobiography of Edward Underhill*, written after 1561

### H His secretary's view on Cranmer

. . . neither fear of losing of promotion, nor hope of gain or winning of favour, could move him to relent or give place unto the truth of his conscience. As experience thereof well appeared, as well in the defence of the true religion against the Six Articles in the parliament, as when he offered to combat with the Duke of Northumberland in King Edward's time . . .

From Ralph Morice: *Anecdotes and Character of Archbishop Cranmer* (c.1565)

### I A Catholic's view on Cranmer [written by a Catholic Archdeacon of Canterbury in Mary's reign]

Doctor Warham being dead Henry bestowed upon Cranmer the archbishopric of Canterbury. Then lo had Cranmer the sweet sop he looked for, that made him so drunk that he knew not nor cared what he did so he might serve the King's pleasure and appetite . . .

. . . neither was there any bearward might more command his bears than the King might command him.

... Only this I will tell you, that in all his life he never showed more inconstancy and mutability ... than at his very end; for whereas he had by writing recanted and revoked his heresies ... whereby if he continued he might have saved his poor soul, lo, suddenly that same day when he saw he should needs die he revolted and reverted with the dog to his pestilent vomit. So this revocation was only for an outward show while he was yet in some hope to get thereby pardon for his temporal life ...

From Nicholas Harpsfield: *Treatise touching the pretended divorce of Henry the Eighth* (undated)

## J   Cranmer at his Trial
### (i) On the Supremacy
I will never consent to the Bishop of Rome; for then should I give myself to the devil; for I have made an oath to the king, and I must obey the king by God's laws. By the scripture, the king is chief, and no foreign person in his own realm above him.
### (ii) On becoming Archbishop
I protest before you all, there was never man came more unwillingly to a bishopric than I did to that.
### (iii) On the Eucharist
Martin: What doctrine taught you when you condemned Lambert the sacramentary in the king's presence in Whitehall?
Cranmer: I maintained then the papists' doctrine ...
Martin: ... And how when king Henry died? ... Then there you defended another doctrine touching the sacrament. ... Then from a Lutheran ye became a Zwinglian, which is the vilest heresy of all ...
Cranmer: I grant that then I believed otherwise than I do now, and so I did until my lord of London, Doctor Ridley, did confer with me, and by sundry persuasions and authorities of doctors drew me quite from my opinion.

Extracts from the trial of Thomas Cranmer, 1555

## K   Cranmer's execution
But that I know for our great friendship and long-continued love you look, even of duty, that I should signify to you of the truth of such things as here chanceth among us, I would not at this time have written to you the unfortunate end and doubtful tragedy of T.C. late Bishop of Canterbury, because I little pleasure take in beholding of such heavy sights. And when they are once overpassed, I like not to rehearse them again, being but a renewing of my woe and doubling my grief. For although his former life and wretched end deserves a greater misery (if any greater might have chanced than chanced unto him), yet setting

aside his offences to God and his country, and beholding the man without his faults, I think there was none that pitied not his case and bewailed his fortune, and feared not his own chance, to see so noble a prelate, so grave a counsellor, of so long-continued honour, after so many dignities, in his old years to be deprived of his estate, adjudged to die and in so painful a death to end his life . . .

His patience in the torment, his courage in dying, if it had been taken either for the glory of God, the wealth of his country, or the testimony of truth, as it was for a pernicious error and subversion of true religion, I could worthily have commended the example and matched it with the fame of any father of ancient time: but seeing that not the death, but the cause and quarrel thereof, commendeth the sufferer, I cannot but much dispraise his obstinate stubbornness and sturdiness in dying, and especially in so evil a cause. Surely his death much grieved every man, but not after one sort. Some pitied to see his body so tormented with the fire raging upon the silly carcass, that counted not of the folly. Other that passed not much of the body, lamented to see him spill his soul wretchedly, without redemption, to be plagued for ever. His friends sorrowed for love, his enemies for pity, strangers for a common kind of humanity whereby we are bound one to another.

Letter from an anonymous Catholic, written two days after the execution

# Questions

**1 a** Why has the artist included the written elements in the portrait in Source A? **(3 marks)**

**b** Compare Source A with Source B. Describe and account for the differences between them. **(4 marks)**

**c** Of what value can portraits such as Sources A and B be to the historian? **(6 marks)**

**2** Comment on the significance for the historian of Source C. **(4 marks)**

**3 a** How do the Prayer Books of 1549 and 1552 (Source E) differ in their treatment of the communion service? **(5 marks)**

**b** What is the significance of these differences? **(5 marks)**

**c** What further information do the other sources provide on the development of Cranmer's beliefs on the Eucharist? **(4 marks)**

**4** Compare the treatment of Cranmer's attitude to Catholics in Sources F and G. Account for any differences. **(6 marks)**

**5** Using your knowledge, comment on how the view expressed in Source J(i) would pose a dilemma for Cranmer in the reign of Mary I? **(3 marks)**

6  'I cannot see in principle why a man's friends are more likely to tell the truth about him than his enemies' (David Starkey). Comment on this remark with reference to these sources on Thomas Cranmer.

**(7 marks)**

7  How adequately do these sources illustrate Cranmer's contribution to the Protestant Reformation?  **(10 marks)**

# 8 THE ELIZABETHAN SETTLEMENT

There was little doubt when Elizabeth came to the throne that she would adopt some form of Protestantism [A-B]. The circumstances of her birth – daughter of Anne Boleyn, whose marriage had been a factor in the break from Rome, and a bastard in the eyes of the Catholic Church – have perhaps been over-emphasised in some explanations of her religious allegiance. (Her mother's marriage to Henry had been declared null and void by Cranmer, and Elizabeth declared a bastard by an English Parliament in 1536.) Of more importance was her upbringing, which included periods in various reformist households and an education that was sympathetic to reform. She had conformed to Catholicism under Mary but on her accession soon gave evidence of her true feelings – appointing Protestant advisers, choosing Protestant preachers to give public sermons and walking out of her own chapel when the bishop saying mass insisted on elevating the host at the consecration when she had told him not to do so.

The question still remained as to what form of Protestantism would be imposed. Would it be the doctrinally conservative supremacy of Henry VIII or the 'full Protestantism' of Edward VI [G]? Nor need it end there. The English Protestants who had gone abroad in Mary's reign had encountered, and in some cases adopted, even more radical ideas. When they returned [C], they brought their ideas with them – on ceremonies, vestments and the role of bishops. There were of course Protestants remaining in England, some, like William Cecil, rapidly appointed to important posts. Less affected by European reformers, they may have wanted a return to the religion of Edward VI's reign.

The Catholics – bishops and leading laymen – also had to be taken into consideration. They might not influence the form of the final settlement but the tactics [E-F] used to bring about that settlement would not succeed unless they were taken into account. Any permanent change in religion would have to be enacted in Parliament and that required cooperation from both the House of Commons and the House of Lords; and in the Lords, at least, the Catholic bishops and peers could, if they turned out in force, command a majority.

This Catholic opposition [H-I] is nowadays seen as a major factor in Elizabeth's tactics. Previously, influenced by the writings of J.E. Neale in the 1960s, it was thought that Elizabeth planned a moderate, possibly interim, settlement but was pushed beyond her intentions by the strength of Protestant feeling demonstrated particularly in the Commons. N.L. Jones, in the 1980s, argued that in fact Elizabeth gained precisely the settlement that she desired, and which she never wanted to change, and that the main threat came from the conservative opposition. They had to be dealt with by the careful construction of bills put forward in Parliament and by ensuring the absence of certain individuals from the Lords.

What was the settlement that resulted from this? Certainly it was Protestant, but how was it regarded by people at the time, both Englishmen and foreigners [J-M]? Who criticised it and why? And, in spite of criticisms, why did it manage to survive?

## A   A description of Princess Elizabeth

His sister, the daughter of the late king by queen Anne, is influenced with the same zeal for the religion of Christ. She not only knows what the true religion is, but has acquired such proficiency in Greek and Latin, that she is able to defend it by the most just arguments and the most happy talent; so that she encounters but few adversaries whom she does not overcome.

John Hooper, the Protestant reformer, to Henry Bullinger, 5 February 1550

## B   An ambassador predicts the future

Such is the state of affairs of the Catholic religion, which are in the more danger, as should my Lady Elizabeth succeed, were she not by nature and education inclined towards the contrary one, she would tend to do the reverse of what the queen has done, this seeming to her a sort of revenge. Besides this, she would think that nothing could render her more popular, independently of her own interest, through the restitution of herself and to the crown of all those revenues amounting to upwards of £60,000, of which the queen has deprived it. And even in case she do not abolish the ceremonies and the use of the sacraments according to the Catholic ritual, they would at least be put back in the state they were left by her father King Henry; and above all she would withdraw the obedience to the Pope, were it solely for the sake of not seeing money go out of the kingdom.

From the report of the Venetian ambassador, May 1557

## C   The reaction of the Bishop of Winchester to Mary's death

I see the wolf coming towards the flock; as at this point I warn you the wolves be coming out of Geneva and other places of Germany, they have sent their books before them full of pestilent doctrine, blasphemy, and heresy to infect the people.

John White, Bishop of Winchester, speaking at Mary's funeral, 14 December 1558

### D The reaction of a layman

I give to the house of Syon £4. Item I give to the Charterhouse 4s 4d. Item I give to the house of Greenwich 4s 4d desiring every one of the said houses to make me a brother of their chapters ... to the said William Page ... a primer both Latin and English. Item I give to John Pencooke of Battle a pair of new prayer beads.

From the will of Walter Fynche of Battle, Sussex, 24 December 1558

### E Advice against compromise

... such times by the mercy of God are restored to your England, when, under the protection of a most godly queen, the liberty of worshipping God in truth will again be granted to godly men. ... May he also grant that the hopes of the faithful, which they have universally begun to entertain respecting the kingdom of England, may be fully realised! ... do not follow their counsels, who, perceiving that popery can neither honestly be defended nor entirely retained, adopt those artifices by which they invent a form of religion of a mixed, uncertain, and doubtful character, and obtrude the same upon the churches under the pretext of evangelical reformation from which the return to papistical superstition and idol-madness is afterwards most easy ... we have now experienced in Germany for some years, to the great detriment of the churches, the extent of influence possessed by men of this character; forasmuch as their counsels appear to the carnal judgement to be full of moderation, and especially adapted to the promotion of concord: and it is likely that the common enemy of our salvation will also find suitable instruments among yourselves, by the aid of which he will endeavour to retain the seeds of popery; which must be firmly resisted with the weapons of Holy Scripture and of the divine word, lest, while we endeavour to avoid giving some small offence at the first beginning, many things be allowed, as if to endure only for a time, which it will afterwards be scarcely possible by any effort, and not without the most grievous struggles, altogether to remove.

The Protestant reformer Rodolph Gualter to Richard Masters, 16 January 1559

### F Elizabeth's tactics: ambiguity, or the middle way?

From the very beginning of her reign Elizabeth has treated all religious questions with so much caution and incredible prudence that she seems both to protect the Catholic religion and at the same time not entirely to condemn or outwardly reject the new reformation. . . . In my opinion, a very prudent action, intended to keep adherents of both creeds in subjection, for the less she ruffles them at the beginning of her reign the more easily will she enthral them later on.

Count von Helfsteein to the Emperor, 16 March 1559

## G   Settlement by Statute

And further be it enacted. . . . That all and singular ministers in any cathedral or parish church or other place . . . shall . . . be bounden to say and use the Matins, Evensong, celebration of the Lord's Supper, and administration of each of the Sacraments, and all their Common and open Prayer, in such order and form as is mentioned in the said book so authorised by Parliament in the said fifth and sixth years of the reign of King Edward the Sixth, with one alteration and addition of certain Lessons to be used on every Sunday in the year, and the form of the Litany altered and corrected, and two sentences only added in the delivery of the Sacrament to the communicants, and none other or otherwise . . .

Provided always and be it enacted, That such ornaments of the Church and of the ministers thereof shall be retained and be in use, as was in the Church of England, by authority of Parliament, in the second year of the reign of King Edward the Sixth, until other order shall be therein taken by the authority of the Queen's Majesty, with the advice of her commissioners . . . for ecclesiastical causes, or of the Metropolitan of this realm: and also that . . . the Queen's Majesty may by the like advice of the said commissioners or Metropolitan ordain and publish such further ceremonies or rites as may be most for the advancement of God's glory, the edifying of his Church and the due reverence of Christ's holy mysteries and sacraments.

From the Act of Uniformity, 1559

## H   The bishops in the House of Lords oppose the settlement

The bishops are a great hindrance to us; for being, as you know, among the leading men in the upper house, and having none there on our side to expose their artifices and confute their falsehoods, they reign as sole monarchs in the midst of weak and ignorant men, and easily overreach our little party, either by their numbers, or their reputation for learning. The queen, meanwhile, though she openly favours our cause, yet is wonderfully afraid of allowing any innovations: this is owing partly to her own friends, by whose advice everything is carried on, and partly to the influence of Count Feria, a Spaniard and Philip's ambassador. She is however prudently, and firmly, and piously following up her purpose, though somewhat more slowly than we could wish. And though the beginnings have hitherto seemed somewhat unfavourable, there is nevertheless reason to hope that all will be well at last. . . .

The queen regards you most highly: she made so much of your letter, that she read it over with the greatest eagerness a second and third time. I doubt not but that your book, when it arrives, will be yet more acceptable.

The Protestant reformer John Jewel to Peter Martyr, 20 March 1559

### I Further obstacles to the settlement
It is to be supposed that when the Pope knows what has happened he will proceed against the Queen and the people here, and it would be of great importance for him to be informed that in the time of Henry VIII the whole Parliament consented without any contradiction whatever except from the bishop of Rochester and Thomas More, whereas now not a single ecclesiastic has agreed to what the Queen has done and of the laymen in the lower chamber and in the upper some opposed on the question of schism, and a great many opposed the heresies.

Count Feria, the Spanish ambassador, to King Philip, 10 May 1559

### J A reaction to the settlement
The news is that in the neighbourhood of Winchester they have refused to receive the church service book, which is the office which these heretics have made up, and the clergy of the diocese had assembled to discuss what they should do. No mass was being said, whereat the congregations were very disturbed.

Bishop Quadra, Spanish ambassador, to Philip II, 27 June 1559

### K The Spanish ambassador reports to Philip II
Some four or five days ago the Queen summoned the Earl of Sussex and told him . . . he had to leave to visit the Emperor at once. . . . He said [that] . . . as to the question of religion he wished to be quite clear about it before he left, because although he was a native born Englishman and knew as well as others what was passing in the country, he was at a loss to state what was the religion that really was observed here. He believed that Her Majesty and the rest of them held by the Augsburg Confession [i.e. were Lutheran] but he saw nevertheless that Calvinism was being preached and being taught nearly everywhere, and he therefore wished the Council to decide about this as it was a point of the highest importance, those who adopted the Augsburg Confession being further removed from Calvinists than from those who professed the ancient religion [i.e. Catholicism]. In fact . . . in the last Parliament here . . . one of the bishops showed himself in favour of the Augsburg creed and was so

much reprehended by the rest of them that the Bishop of London had gone so far as to say that no one ought to speak to him, and quoted St Paul publicly to this end.

De Silva, the Spanish ambassador, to Philip II, 26 April 1567

**L   The rising of the northern earls [an account written from York]**
I perceive Her Majesty is to believe that the force of her subjects of this country should not increase, and be able to match with the rebels; but it is easy to find the cause. There are not ten gentlemen in all this country that favour her proceedings in the cause of religion. The common people are ignorant, superstitious, and altogether blinded with the old popish doctrine, and therefore so favour the cause which the rebels make the colour of their rebellion, that, though their persons be here with us, their hearts are wholly with them. And no doubt all this country had wholly rebelled if, at the beginning, my Lord Lieutenant had not wisely and stoutly handled the matter. If we should go to the field with this northern force only, they would fight faintly; for if the father be on this side, the son is on the other; and one brother with us and the other with the rebels.

Sir Ralph Sadler to Sir William Cecil, 6 December 1569

**M   Compromise**
As for the manner of their service in church and their prayers, except that they say them in the English tongue, one can still recognise a great part of the Mass . . . for they still keep the Epistle and the Gospel, the *Gloria in Excelsis Deo*, the Creed. They sing the psalms in English and at certain hours of the day, as at matins and vespers, they use organs and music. The canons wear the amice and surplice, as also the others, and have copes, and it seems, saving for the images, that there is little difference between their ceremonies and those of the Church of Rome.

From a report of the French ambassador, de Maisse, 1597

# Questions

1 Comment on the value of Source A as evidence of Elizabeth's personal religion.                                                    **(4 marks)**

2 What reasons are given in Source B for Elizabeth's reversal of Mary's religious policy?                                               **(3 marks)**

3 a Using your own knowledge, explain the reference to 'Geneva' in Source C.                                                          **(2 marks)**

   b In Source D what is meant by 'House of Syon', 'Charterhouse' and 'House of Greenwich'?                                          **(2 marks)**

**4** How and why do Sources E and F differ in their attitude to a 'middle way' in achieving a settlement? **(6 marks)**

**5** What does Source K reveal of the nature of the Elizabethan Settlement? **(4 marks)**

**6** How would the author of Source E have reacted to the comment made in Source M? **(4 marks)**

**7** Using these sources and your own knowledge, consider the evidence for and against the likelihood of England remaining a Catholic country on Elizabeth's succession. **(10 marks)**

ELIZABETH I AND THE CHURCH

Despite complaints about some of Elizabeth's personal preferences in religion, such as her insisting on keeping a crucifix and candlesticks in her chapel or her dislike of married clergy, nobody really doubted her basic commitment to the Protestant Church. Where criticisms could arise, it was over the way she sometimes seemed to take advantage of her position in the Church. As Supreme Governor she had the responsibility of choosing the bishops and senior officers of the Church, and although this had also been largely the practice of her predecessors before the Reformation, she no longer had to make even a token gesture to another authority as previous monarchs had to the Pope. The dissolution of the monasteries and transfer of their property to laymen had also meant the transfer of the monasteries' rights to enjoy the income of many parishes while appointing priests on a salary to minister in those parishes. This income and right of appointment were now enjoyed by many laymen and like Elizabeth they took full advantage of it. In such a situation it was all too easy for Elizabeth and her subjects to regard the Church as a source of wealth and of rewards for loyal servants [A-C, E-F].

This could also make the position of the bishops very difficult [G]. They relied on royal patronage [H-I], accepted royal supremacy, and were generally loyal servants. How then could they react if they disagreed with the Queen [E]? Or if they felt that they did not get enough support in carrying out their duties? They were often called upon by Elizabeth to enforce certain aspects of the settlement but did not always think that they received enough moral or practical support.

What of the bishops themselves? They were a key element in the Church and the quality of a church is influenced, and often judged, by the quality of its bishops. On what basis can we judge their quality – as administrators, royal servants, theologians or pastors [J]? How did they see their role with regard to the Queen and the people?

**A    An appeal against the Act for the Exchange of Bishops' Lands of 1559 [which allowed the Queen to exchange the lands of a vacant see for royal sources of income in the same see]**

Most humbly sheweth your excellent Majesty, your lowly orators and loving subjects we underwritten, that like as your most noble father of immortal memory, King Henry VIII, and your most godly and noble brother, King Edward VI, in their princely zeal which they bare to the state of Christ's faith did much tender the advancement of learning by cherishing of students and encouraging of ministers, whereby they were the more able to do their duties to God, and to serve the necessity of the realm, by which their royal and princely affection they purchased perpetual fame and praise, as well within their own realms as throughout all Christendom: so we trust undoubtedly that your Grace, being endued with the benefits of knowledge far above any of your noble progenitors, will be inclined no less to the maintenance of learning for the setting forth of Christ's true religion, now for want of true ministers in great jeopardy of decay. In respect whereof we trust that your Highness' gracious disposition will yet stay and remit this present alteration and exchange (as we suppose in our consciences under reformation of your great wisdom), not meet to proceed for the inconveniences thereof now partly perceived like to ensue, and upon such good grounds and reasons as we could particularly describe in writing if your Highness' pleasure were to admit us to the declaration of the same.

And yet, lest we should appear not to consider your Highness' manifold and great charges daily sustained, in most humble wise we five underwritten, for us and the province of Canterbury, do offer to give unto the same yearly amongst us one annual pension of one thousand marks during our lives and continuance in the bishoprics for and in consideration of the said exchange.

Letter from Matthew Parker, Archbishop-elect of Canterbury, and the bishops-elect of London, Ely, Hereford and Chichester (October 1559)

## B   The Queen's response
Whereas the archbishop elect of Canterbury and the other elect bishops of London, Ely, Hereford, and Chichester remain unconsecrated, by reason that the exchange is not finished between us and them, for certain temporalities, according to the power given us by a statute in the last Parliament, whereby we be informed the state ecclesiastical in the province of Canterbury and the rest of the said dioceses remaineth without government; our pleasure is that ye shall with all expedition proceed to finish the said exchange.

Queen Elizabeth to the Lord Treasurer and the Barons of the Exchequer, 26 October 1559

## C   Bishops and their finances
As to your expressing your hopes that our bishops will be consecrated without any superstitious and offensive ceremonies, you mean, I suppose, without oil, without the chrism, without the tonsure. And you are not mistaken; for the sink would indeed have been emptied to no

purpose, if we had suffered those dregs to settle at the bottom. Those oily, shaven, portly hypocrites we have sent back to Rome from whence we first imported them: for we require our bishops to be pastors, labourers, and watchmen. And that this may the more readily be brought to pass, the wealth of the bishops is now diminished and reduced to a reasonable amount, to the end that, being relieved from that royal pomp and courtly bustle, they may with greater ease and diligence employ their leisure in attending to the flock of Christ.

The Protestant reformer John Jewel to Josiah Simler, 2 November 1559

### D   The Bishop of Coventry and Lichfield pleads poverty

In most humble and obedient wise sueth unto your highness your poor and daily orator Thomas . . . bishop of Coventry and Lichfield, That whereas your grace's highness hath bestowed upon your said suppliant the afore-named bishopric and he at the taking upon him the said office of ministry, being a man of poor estate and calling and since that time put to such great charges . . . and finding his bishopric [also] in that case and state . . . may it please your Majesty's highness . . . to release [your suppliant] of some part of his first fruits and especially of the first payment . . . or else he shall be able, neither to pay any part of his debts, which to him is a great grief, neither to make necessary provision for housekeeping, nor to keep any house at all, which he judgeth will renown much to the slander of the gospel, whereby he shall be unable either to serve God or your highness as his duty and will is.

Thomas Bentham, Bishop of Coventry and Lichfield, to Queen Elizabeth, 9 September 1560

### E   Elizabeth and the Bishop of Ely [when he refused to give some of his bishopric's property to Sir Christopher Hatton]

Proud Prelate, You know what you were before I made you what you are now. If you do not immediately comply with my request, I will unfrock you by God, Elizabeth.

Elizabeth to the Bishop of Ely, 1573

### F   Elizabeth and the Bishop of Winchester

We require therefore a speedy lease [for Sir Francis Carew] such as shall reward his long service and be least hurtful to the bishopric.

Elizabeth to Thomas Bilson on his appointment as Bishop of Winchester, 1596

### G   Exploiting the system [written by Queen Elizabeth's godson]

[On Thomas Godwin, Bishop of Bath and Wells] Being, as I said, aged and diseased, and lame of the gout, he married . . . a widow of London. A chief favourite of that time Sir Walter Raleigh . . . had laboured to get the manor of Banwell from the bishopric, and . . . now hearing of this intempestive marriage, took advantage thereof, caused it to be told to the Queen (knowing how much she misliked such matches) and instantly pursued the bishop with letters and mandates for the manor of Banwell for 100 years. The good bishop, not expecting such a sudden tempest, was greatly perplexed, yet a while he held out and endured many sharp messages from the Queen, of which myself carried him one, delivered me by my Lord of Leicester. . . . The conclusion . . . was this, that to satisfy his persecutors and to save Banwell he was fain to part with Wilscombe for 99 years . . . and so purchased his peace. Thus the bishopric as well as the bishop were punished.

From Sir John Harrington: *A Supplie or Addicion to Bishop Godwin's Catalogue of Bishops*, written between 1603 and 1612

### H  A clergyman seeks promotion
Good my lord, if the deanery of Winchester be not already swallowed up, let me among the rest of the small fishes have a snatch at the bait; if it be gone, I beseech your good lordship cast a hook for the deanery of Durham that when Mr Horne is sped of a bishopric I may have that to serve God, my country and the Queen's Majesty in.

John Aylmer to Robert Dudley (a leading courtier and later Earl of Leicester), 12 August 1559

### I  The Bishop of Coventry and Lichfield appeals to the Vice-Chamberlain
In most considerate wise my duty remembered to your honour these may be to desire the same so favourably to accept this bearer Mr Reniger as to help to prefer his suit unto the Queen. . . . He was at Zurich when I and others were there also: for which cause I think him meet to be preferred. And yet chiefly I write this much because that I do know his learning and living to deserve good preferment.

Thomas Bentham, Bishop of Coventry and Lichfield, to Sir Francis Knollys, Vice-Chamberlain to the Queen, 1 July 1560

### J  An Elizabethan epitaph in Southwell Minster
The body of him who lies here was not of humble birth and lived with rank and in great state but the example he set was greater, having filled two bishoprics he was at length promoted to be archbishop, having attained these honours at a high price with his virtues and deserts. He was a man above all men free from malice and vindictiveness, open and

free of flattery, very liberal and compassionate, most hospitable, easy going and proud without it being a vice. He lived no less worthily than he taught others to do and devoted himself in preaching the gospel, being assiduous in this task to the end. No one could go away from listening to his sermons without being the better for them. He wished for eloquence and it was evident in him. Conscious of his own hard labours he despised the idlers. He encouraged learning for the benefits it brought. He upheld Church possessions as anything dedicated to God deserved to be. By your favour with Elizabeth the most illustrious of mortals, oh venerable man, you were able to save this church in which you yourself lie from despoil. You were a notable example of the chances of life who however much you had to bear endured all ills great and many with imperturbable spirit – prison, exile, loss of much good fortune and above all the hardest thing for an innocent mind to bear, most malicious slanders: and in one thing alone was your wish unfulfilled, the shedding of your own blood in support of your belief in Christ. And now after such fluctuation in prosperity and so many contests against hostility, being tired of life you have at length achieved the goal of perpetual rest in your search for God, rejoice evermore for your toils are acceptable to God instead of your blood being shed. Go, reader, do not think it enough to know these things but copy them.

From the tomb of Edwin Sandys, Archbishop of York, who died in 1588

# Questions

**1** Comment on the language and arguments used in Source A. What do they tell us about the bishops' attitude towards Elizabeth I and how they feel she might be influenced? **(5 marks)**

**2** Compare Sources A, B, C and D as evidence for the financial problems faced by the bishops in Elizabeth I's reign. **(6 marks)**

**3** Use Sources E, F and G to analyse the relationship between Elizabeth I and the bishops. **(6 marks)**

**4** What picture do Sources G, H and I give of relations between the bishops and the court? **(6 marks)**

**5** With particular reference to Source J, comment on the value of epitaphs to the historian. (Reference should be made to other sources in this chapter.) **(7 marks)**

**6** Using these sources, and your own knowledge, discuss the proposition that Elizabeth gained more from her supremacy than did the English Church. **(10 marks)**

# 10 THE ROYAL SUPREMACY

In the areas of doctrine and discipline the reigns of Henry VIII, Edward VI and Elizabeth I present a number of differences, but one important feature common to the three of them was the royal supremacy. First introduced in the 1530s, it became the essential feature of the established Protestant Church [A-C].

It was important as the basis for enforcing particular religious policies. Although ultimately doctrine was based on the Bible, the monarch's authority was necessary to impose it on the country and to make decisions on what kind of organisation and liturgy the Church should have. This applied whether the monarch was a knowledgeable though unpredictable theologian like Henry, a young enthusiast like Edward, or a cautious, well-educated woman like Elizabeth – he or she exercised an authority that had to be obeyed. Such a teaching had its problems of course. What does a supporter of the supremacy do if a particular supreme head does not act in accordance with his other religious beliefs? What are the limits of active or passive resistance?

This could be a real problem because royal supremacy was not just a convenient way of getting religious reforms implemented. For many people it was an essential element in the Church. There were various ways of justifying this view [D]. One was to point to the example of the Old Testament kings who, it was claimed, exercised both a religious and a secular authority. New Testament references to the obedience due to all rulers were also brought into play. History provided further justification [E]. Attention was drawn to the actions of early Christian emperors in summoning and presiding over Church Councils [J]. That Constantine, the first of these emperors, had a British mother was an added advantage in giving the claim a more localised flavour. For many, such theories were probably unnecessary and royal supremacy simply became part of the tradition of obedience that was an accepted part of people's thinking.

But although supremacy remained a constant feature, did its practice change? Would different rulers adopt different approaches or prompt different reactions? In the case of Edward VI, for example, how far could a minor be expected to exercise the supremacy and, if he could not exercise it in person, did anyone else have the right to exercise it on his behalf? The conservative Stephen Gardiner argued that there should be a stop to further reform until the King came of age. When Elizabeth came to the throne, did the fact that she was a woman have any influence on her role in the Church [F-I]?

Finally, was the supremacy something inherent in the royal dignity or could the monarch somehow be made supreme and, if so, by whom [K-M]? What role did Parliament have to play in this?

## A Henry VIII's Supremacy

Albeit the King's Majesty justly and rightfully is and oweth to be the supreme head of the Church of England, and so is recognised by the clergy of this realm in their convocations: yet nevertheless for corroboration and confirmation thereof . . . Be it enacted by the authority of this present Parliament that the King our sovereign lord, his heirs and successors . . . shall be taken, accepted and reputed the only supreme head in earth of the Church of England. . . . And that our said sovereign lord . . . shall have full power and authority from time to time to visit, repress, redress, reform, order, correct, restrain and amend all such errors, heresies, abuses, offences, contempts and enormities, whatsoever they be . . .

From the Act of Supremacy, 1534

## B Stephen Gardiner comments on the Act of Supremacy

Wherein there is no newly invented matter wrought, only their will was to have the power pertaining to a prince by God's law to be the more clearly expressed with a more fit term to express it by, namely, for this purpose to withdraw that counterfeit vain opinion out of common people's minds which the false pretensed power of the Bishop of Rome had for the space of certain years blinded them withall, to the great impeachment of the king's authority, which all men are bounden to wish and to their uttermost power see kept safe, restored, and defended from wrongs.

From Stephen Gardiner: *Concerning True Obedience* (1535)

## C   The title page to the Great Bible, first published in 1539

## D  A new image
### (i) From Moses . . .
And Moses went up unto God and the Lord called unto him out of the mountain . . . And the Lord said unto Moses, Lo, I come unto thee in a thick cloud that the people may hear when I speak with thee, and believe thee for ever . . . And Moses went down from the mount unto the people.

Exodus 19: iii,ix,xiv

### (ii) . . . to Henry VIII
Is it not convenient and most meet that yearly for ever, in memory that our Saviour Christ, by his Moses, Your Majesty, hath delivered us out of the bondage of the most wicked pharaoh of all pharaohs, the Bishop of Rome . . . we keep a solemn feast thereof, to give God laud and thanks therefore?

From Richard Morison: *A Discourse Touching the Reformation of the Laws of England*, written by 1542

## E  Looking for evidence
### (i) A fictitious letter [Lucius did not exist and the letter was written in the thirteenth century, it appeared twice in a collection of authorities compiled for Henry VIII in the early 1530s]
You seek from us Roman and imperial laws to be sent to you, which you wish to use in the kingdom of Britain. . . . You have received recently by divine mercy the law and faith of Christ in the kingdom of Britain. You have with you in the kingdom both books of scripture, from which by God's grace with the counsel of your realm take a law, and by that law through God's sufferance rule your kingdom of Britain. For you are vicar of God in your kingdom . . . The omnipotent God grant you so to rule the kingdom of Britain that you may reign with him eternally, whose vicar you are in the said realm.

From a letter said to have been written to King Lucius of Britain from Pope Eleutherius, AD 167

### (ii) A Chronicle of England
For all such old monuments as we had, Mr Secretary hath them two years ago. . . . He had . . . a Chronicle of England the author unknown. . . . One notable story was in the Chronicle; how after the Saxons conquered, continual war remained betwixt the Britons (then inhabitants of the realm) and the Saxons, the Britons being Christians, and the Saxons pagans. As occasion served they sometimes treated of peace, and then met together, communed together, and did eat and drink together. But after that by the means of Augustine the Saxons

became Christians in such sort as Augustine had taught them, the Britons would not after that neither eat nor drink with them, nor yet salute them, because they corrupted with superstition, images, and idolatry, the true religion of Christ, which the Britons had reserved pure among them from the time of King Lucius.

Bishop Davies of St David's to Archbishop Parker, March 1565

## F   Women and Supremacy
... for a woman to call herself head of that multitude which constitutes the church is forbidden by divine as well as natural law ...

Cardinal Pole to Mary I, 1 December 1553

## G   Elizabeth I's Supremacy
... that such jurisdictions, privileges, superiorities and pre-eminences spiritual and ecclesiastical, as by any spiritual or ecclesiastical power or authority hath heretofore been or may lawfully be exercised or used for the visitation of the ecclesiastical state and persons, and for the reformation, order and correction of the same ... shall for ever by authority of this present parliament be united and annexed to the imperial crown of this realm.

   And that your Highness, your heirs and successors ... shall have full power and authority by virtue of this act ... to assign, name and authorise ... such person or persons ... as your Majesty, your heirs or successors, shall think meet to exercise ... all manner of jurisdictions, privileges and pre-eminences in any wise touching or concerning any spiritual or ecclesiastical jurisdiction within these your realms ...

From the Act of Supremacy, 1559

## H   The Oath from the Act of Supremacy
I, *A.B.*, do utterly testify and declare in my conscience that the Queen's Highness is the only supreme governor of this realm ... as well in all spiritual or ecclesiastical things or causes as temporal ...

The oath to be taken by all office-holders, from the Act of Supremacy, 1559

## I   Title page of the Bishops' Bible, 1569

## J   An Elizabethan bishop's appeal to his Queen

The first is that you would refer all these ecclesiastical matters which touch religion, or the doctrine and discipline of the church, unto the bishops and divines of your realm, according to the example of all godly Christian emperors and princes of all ages . . .

The second petition . . . is this: that, when you deal in matters of faith and religion . . . you would not use to pronounce so resolutely and peremptorily, as if from authority, as ye may do in civil and extern matters . . .

Archbishop Grindal to Queen Elizabeth, 1576

## K Propaganda

### (i) A picture by Girolamo da Treviso the Younger, painted for Henry VIII, *c.*1540

### (ii) Queen Elizabeth – an initial C from the 1563 edition of John Foxe *Acts and Monuments*

**L   Royal Supremacy on display**
**(i) Tivetshall, Norfolk [the arms of Queen Elizabeth in the chancel arch; before the Reformation this space would have been occupied by a large crucifix flanked by statues of Mary and John the Evangelist]**

### (ii) Wix, Essex

Paid for pulling down the rood loft and setting up of the Scriptures [and] . . . the King's Majesty's Arms £4 12s 6d.

From the Churchwardens' Accounts, Wandsworth Church, for 1552.

. . . a cloth stained and written with the scripture, the King's Majesty's Arms in the midst, which cloth is hanging upon the candlebeam [i.e. from the rood loft].

Inventory from Wix church, Essex, 1552

## Questions

1   According to Sources A and B what was the justification for Henry's claim to be Supreme Head and why was parliamentary legislation thought to be necessary? **(3 marks)**

**2** What biblical image of Henry VIII is presented in Sources C and D, and how is this done? **(4 marks)**

**3** How does Source C demonstrate the importance of Henry VIII in the English Church? **(6 marks)**

**4** What is the significance of the documents in Source E in the context of the royal supremacy? **(6 marks)**

**5** Comment on the image of Elizabeth I presented in Source I. **(5 marks)**

**6** What messages are put over in Sources K(i) and (ii) and in what ways? **(7 marks)**

**7** What is the value of Sources L(i) and (ii) to an historian of this period? **(6 marks)**

**8** With particular reference to the sources, comment on the possible difference between the supremacy claimed and exercised by Henry VIII and the supremacy claimed and exercised by Elizabeth I. **(8 marks)**

# 11 PURITANISM IN ELIZABETH'S REIGN

Once the religious settlement had been made by the Acts of Uniformity and Supremacy Elizabeth was determined that it should not be changed and every so often harried her bishops into ensuring full conformity with the decisions of 1559. Others saw it in a very different light and believed 1559 had been a missed opportunity. They were willing to accept that a quick Protestant settlement had been necessary but regarded it as an interim measure, suited to the immediate circumstances, but not the Church of God as it should be permanently established.

Some of these critics felt they had seen the Church of God when they were in exile during Mary's reign. They returned with experience of the reformed churches of the continent and sought to introduce their ideals into the new Church of England. Other critics emerged from those who had stayed in England. Driven underground, they had only been able to survive as small independent congregations and now wished to continue this separate existence rather than be drawn into a church of bishops and ceremonies that they associated with Catholicism [G]. The moderation of the settlement – undoubtedly Protestant in doctrine but with concessions aimed if not at Catholics then at least at the conservatives – served only to alienate those who wanted a pure church untainted by compromise.

These seekers after further reform were the people we know as Puritans. It would be difficult to summarise their demands, which varied according to time, place and individual, or the kind of people they were [E-F]. They came from every class and even bishops can be accounted Puritans under some definitions. For example, Edmund Grindal, as Bishop of London, took action against a separatist group in the 1560s for the sake of the unity of the Church although expressing some sympathy for their opinions; but in 1576 his refusal to suppress the prophesyings or exercises [C-D] that Elizabeth so disliked resulted in his virtual suspension from office as Archbishop of Canterbury until his death in 1583. One of the historian's main problems with Puritanism then is to find out just what a Puritan was.

Elizabeth's antipathy towards Puritanism is fairly clear; but how can it be explained? Was it a distrust of change or did she simply dislike what she imagined Puritanism to be? Why did she see them as a threat to the civil government as much as to the religious establishment? How far did the methods used by the Puritans to achieve their aims, as much as the aims themselves, prompt suspicions of their motives?

However defined, Puritanism had quietened down by the 1590s and some explanation of this is also necessary. Many people consider it to be linked with an apparent lessening of the Catholic threat or a conscious retreat from extremism or a surrender to a successful campaign by the established Church. Certainly, although it did not disappear, by the end of the reign most Puritans seem to have found a place within the Church.

## A    A permanent settlement? [comments on the Act of Uniformity]

I trust we will not linger here for long, for the parliament draweth towards an end. The last book of service is gone through with a proviso to retain the ornaments which were used in the first and second year of King Edward, until it please the queen to take other order for them; our gloss upon this text is, that we shall not be forced to use them, but that others in the meantime shall not convey them away, but that they may remain for the queen.

Edwin Sandys, later Bishop of Worcester, to Matthew Parker, later Archbishop of Canterbury, 30 April 1559

## B    A plea for toleration

As touching your letters, wherein your Honour writeth that her Majesty is fully bent to remove all those that cannot be persuaded to conform themselves to all the orders established, it grieveth our souls very much, considering what desolation is like to come to the poor flock of Christ, who shall be thereby bereaved of so many excellent pastors that dare not yield to that conformity. . . . For our own parts, although we do and fully will yield unto our sovereign prince our bodies, goods, and lives, yet herein we dare not yield to this conformity of ceremonies . . . dare not yield to those ceremonies that be so far from edifying and building up the church that they have rent in sunder and miserably torn to pieces this our church . . .

. . . we dare not yield in these things, and yet during the time that we have been in our calling, we never much busied ourselves with them in our sermons, but diligently have laboured to teach our flocks salvation in Jesus Christ, repentance from dead works, true and unfeigned obedience to our godly and gracious prince, in God and for God labouring always to keep the peace and quietness of the church in the bond of the spirit . . .

Now whereas . . . the Queen . . . is hereupon incensed that we will be obedient to no laws, that we would be lords and kings ourselves, that we would pull the crown from her head and sword out of her hand, that we would erect a new popedom: To put her Majesty out of doubt of the untruth of these, and to testify of our true loyalty . . . we take the Lord

God ... to record unto our consciences that we acknowledge from the bottom of our hearts her Highness to be our lawful queen, placed by God over us for our good and wealth. We give God most humble and hearty thanks for her happy government over us. We pray in our public sermons weekly and in our private prayers daily for this prosperous government of her Majesty's over us. We renounce all foreign government and acknowledge her Majesty's title of supremacy to be lawful and just. Unto this her Highness' lawful government, we acknowledge ourselves, bodies, goods, lands, and life, in all obedience to be subject. We detest all heresies, as well of the old as those which Satan hath raised up in our days. As Anabaptistry, the heresy of the Libertines, the family of love, and all puritanism and such like ...

There be already 19 or 20 godly exercises of preaching and catechising put down in this city by the displacing of those preachers. The excellent estate of so happy a city beginneth already hereby to be wonderfully altered from her former comely beauty to tears and mourning, when she sees her godly pastors violently pulled from her ...

If you can do anything with our bishop, move him to be more earnest with the papists, enemies to God and our prince ... while he is busied against good Christians, these enemies gather strength, seeing all the force of law bent against the true professors and toucheth not them.

A Petition from six Norwich ministers, 25 September 1576 (possibly to Lord Burghley)

## C The popularity of exercises

In many of our archdeaconries we have an exercise lately begun, which for the most part is called a prophecy or conference, and erected only for the examination or trial of the diligence of the clergy in their study of holy scriptures. Howbeit such is the thirsty desire of the people in these days to hear the word of God, that they also have as it were with zealous violence intruded themselves among them (but as hearers only), to come by more knowledge through their presence at the same ... and as it is used in some places weekly, in others once in fourteen days, in divers monthly and elsewhere twice a year, so it is a notable spur unto all the ministers thereby to apply their books, which otherwise (as in times past) would give themselves to hawking, hunting, tables, cards, dice, tippling at the alehouse, shooting of matches and other such like vanities. ... But alas! as Satan the author of all mischief hath in sundry manners heretofore hindered the erection and maintenance of many good things, so in this he hath stirred up adversaries of late ... who have ... procured the suppression of these conferences.

From William Harrison: *A Description of England*, 1586–7

### D   Elizabeth prohibits exercises

We hear to our great grief that in sundry parts of our realm there are no small number of persons presuming to be teachers and preachers of the church . . . which, contrary to our laws . . . do daily devise . . . sundry new rites and forms in the church, as well by their unauthorised preaching, readings, and ministering the sacraments, as by procuring unlawfully of assemblies, and great numbers of our people out of their ordinary parishes, and from places far distant, to be hearers of their disputations and new devised opinions, upon points of divinity far unmeet for vulgar people: which manner of innovation they in some places term prophesying, and in some other places, exercises. By which manner of assemblies great numbers of our people, especially the vulgar sort, meet to be otherwise occupied with honest labour for their living, are brought to idleness, and seduced; and in manner schismatically divided among themselves into variety of dangerous opinions, and manifestly thereby encouraged to the violation of our laws, and to the breach of common order.

We therefore . . . do charge and command you that no manner of person be suffered within your diocese to preach, teach, read, or exercise any function in the church, but such as shall be lawfully approved and licensed . . .

And, furthermore, considering for the great abuses that have been in sundry places of our realm, by reason of the aforesaid assemblies, called exercises; we will and straitly charge you that you do cause the same forthwith to cease, and not to be used . . .

An order from Queen Elizabeth to the bishops of England, May 1577

### E   A Puritan petition to the Queen

That every archbishop and bishop of this Church . . . if it be found . . . that the office of the archbishop or bishop, as it is now, is both necessary and profitable for the Church . . . shall . . . have assigned . . . unto him, by the same authority by which he is chosen archbishop or bishop, eight, ten, twelve, or more preaching pastors, doctors and deacons . . . together with some other grave and godly men of worship or justices of the peace within that shire . . . and that the said archbishop and bishop shall, with them and by their counsel, advise and consent, hear and determine every cause ecclesiastical which is now used to be heard before any archbishop and bishop . . .

And that . . . every pastor resident on his charge . . . shall by the advice and direction of the bishop of the diocese, and of his associates, present to the said bishop and his associates, four, six or eight inhabitants of his parish, such as shall be thought . . . meet to be the associates and seniors . . . with the said pastor, to govern his said parish with him. . . .

That neither the said archbishops. . . nor the bishops . . . do hereafter, by their sole and private authority, make and publish any injunctions touching religion or church government . . .

And to the end that the said bishops may hereafter do that office which shall be committed to them the more sincerely, we desire that all they . . . may be delivered from the burden of all wordly pomp, honour and charge . . . and that they also be set so free from the administration of all civil causes and offices, that they may wisely apply themselves to the labour of the gospel and ecclesiastical function in diligence and sincerity . . .

From a petition to the Queen, 1585

## F   Further Puritan demands

Most humbly beseecheth your excellent Majesty, your faithful and obedient subjects, the Lords and Commons of this your Highness' realm of England . . .

So as when it pleased God of his gracious goodness toward this realm to place your most excellent Majesty in the throne of the same, your Highness . . . was enforced by the necessity of sudden change to be made, for the time to revive and restore such former laws and statutes concerning the reformation of the church as had been made by your said noble father and brother; and for the suppressing of the former popish laws, Latin service, and ceremonies, your Highness established a certain form of church government and common prayers, and caused certain penal statutes to be made for the strict observation of the same.

So it is, most gracious Sovereign, that since that time, the light of God's glorious gospel increasing daily by means of your Highness' long, peaceable and blessed reign, learned and zealous men have, as well out of the holy Word of God as by the example of other best reformed churches, observed divers imperfections, corruptions and repugnancies with the Word of God yet continued in the order and discipline of this Church and in the Book of Common Prayer and Ordination of the Ministers appointed for the same. For whereas our Saviour Christ hath set up in his Church for the building up of his saints and for the work of the ministry, pastors and teachers, who being wholly occupied in the things pertaining to God and watching over the souls of men, must be able and apt to teach and give a continual attendance upon that flock whereof the Holy Ghost hath made them overseers . . . And besides hath appointed that in every congregation there should be elders, whose office is in having a more special eye upon the life and manners of every one within their charge, and deacons for distributing of the church alms among the poor. To which pastors, teachers and elders he hath further committed the guidance of his Church . . . that they, by common

89

consent, might direct all the affairs and business of the same by providing for the outward order and comeliness thereof, according to the general rules in the Word of God, by choosing and ordaining all such as are called to any public place of service in the Church . . .

For teachers, elders, and deacons our church lacketh altogether . . . Contrariwise it doth embrace a calling of lord bishops not agreeable to the Word of God, and yet untruly pretended to come from the apostles; which bishops, bearing the state and titles of lords and princes, and employed in civil causes, have no particular congregation whereon they do attend, but exercise a superiority forbidden by our Saviour Christ over their fellow ministers . . .

Furthermore, the said Book of Common Prayer and Ordination of Ministers differeth from the simplicity and sincerity of God's service and from the example of all reformed churches . . . for not yielding whereunto, a great number of your Majesty's most loving and dutiful subjects . . . have under pretence of order and conformity, and by hard construction of laws intended only against the obstinate favourers of the wicked doctrine and superstition of the See of Rome, have been from time to time grievously punished and molested . . .

That it may be enacted by your Majesty with the assent of the Lords and Commons in this present parliament assembled, and by the authority of the same that the book hereunto annexed . . . may be from henceforth authorised, put in use, and practised, throughout all your Majesty's dominions . . .

From A Bill for the further reformation of the Church, offered with the book in the Parliament, 1587

### G   Attacks on the bishops
Chark, in a *clerum* at St Mary's before the University [of Cambridge] had roundly condemned the hierarchy of this church . . . laying down these two bold positions:

These offices of bishop, archbishop, metropolitan, patriarch and finally of pope, were introduced into the Church by Satan.

Among ministers of the Church, it is not necessary for one to be superior to another.

1572, quoted in G.W. Prothero: *Select Statutes and other Constitutional Documents* (1913)

### H   A Puritan pamphlet, one of many printed secretly
Therefore no Lord Bishop (I pray thee, good Martin, speak out, if ever thou didst speak out that her Majesty and the Council may hear thee) is to be tolerated in any Christian commonwealth . . .

Our Lord Bishops . . . are petty Antichrists, petty popes, proud prelates, intolerable withstanders of reformation, enemies of the gospel and most covetous wretched priests . . .

But, Brother Winchester . . . in another [sermon] which he preached at court . . . he protested before God and the congregation where he stood that there was not in the world at this day: nay, there had not been since the Apostles' time such a flourishing estate of a Church as we have now in England. Is it any marvel that we have so many swine, dumb dogs, non-residents with their journeymen the hedge-priests, so many lewd livers, as thieves, murderers, adulterers, drunkards, cormorants, rascals, so many ignorant atheistical dolts, so many covetous, popish bishops in our ministry – and so many and so monstrous corruptions in our Church and yet likely to have no redress: Seeing our impudent, shameless and wainscot-faced bishops, like beasts, contrary to the knowledge of all men and against their consciences, dare in the ears of her Majesty, affirm all to be well, where there is nothing but sores and blisters, yea, where the grief is even deadly at the heart. Nay, says my Lord of Winchester (like a monstrous hypocrite, for he is a very dunce . . .) I have said it, I do say it and I have said it.

From 'Martin Marprelate': *The Epistle*, 1588

## I Disputing with Puritans

I am fully of the opinion, that the hope which many men have conceived of the spoil of bishops' livings, of the subversion of cathedral churches, and of a havoc to be made of all the churches' revenues, is the chiefest and most principal cause of the greatest schisms that we have at this day in our church. . . . The doctrine of the Church of England is pure and holy; the government thereof, both in respect of Her Majesty and of our bishops is lawful and godly; the Book of Common Prayer containeth nothing in it contrary to the Word of God. . . . There is no man living, as I suppose, able to show where there was any church planted ever since the apostles' time, but there bishops had authority over the rest of the ministry.

From Richard Bancroft's sermon, preached at St Paul's Cross, 9 February 1589

## J A Puritan patron

God . . . grant that that exercise may be speedily set up again, the rather by your good means. Wherein I believe your Lordship shall do one of the best services, both to God and your country, that ever you did, for it was undoubtedly without exception counted the best exercise in this realm. . . . For your Lordship's well deserving towards the learned ministers, specially those that of long time have been troubled about the unprofitable ceremonies (for the other could shift well enough for themselves) I can be a witness . . . and that I never knew no man better bent to the setting forth of God's glory and help of such as were the unfeigned professors thereof than you showed yourself at many times when it pleased your Lordship to talk with me.

Thomas Wood to the Earl of Leicester, 7 September 1576

# Questions

**1** What view of the 1559 settlement is put forward in Source A? **(3 marks)**

**2** Compare Sources C and D in their comments on exercises. How and why do they differ? **(6 marks)**

**3** Comment on the style and language of Source H. **(5 marks)**

**4** Compare Sources G and H as evidence for the seriousness of the Puritan threat to the established Church. **(6 marks)**

**5** How do the demands in Source F contrast with the statements made in Source I? **(6 marks)**

**6 a** What motive does Bancroft identify in Source I for Puritan activity? **(2 marks)**

  **b** To what extent is Bancroft a reliable source? **(4 marks)**

**7** To what extent do these sources support the view that the Puritan movement was a threat to order and authority in society? **(8 marks)**

**8** Using your own knowledge, and with reference to the sources, how far is it possible to arrive at a working definition of a 'Puritan'? (Consider beliefs and the kind of people who might be considered to be Puritans.) **(12 marks)**

# 12 CATHOLICISM IN ELIZABETH'S REIGN

On the day of Elizabeth's accession Catholicism was the religion of England; when she died in 1603 anti-Catholicism [B-E] had become the norm for most of the country. Early in Elizabeth's reign she felt a policy of indifference would cause Catholicism to wither away from neglect; in 1603 it still remained as the religion of a small but significant minority that could draw support from all classes.

How was it that the fortunes of Catholicism changed in this way? For many people Catholicism was simply a byword for treason. To some extent this was due to the Protestant authorities who had made the practice of Catholicism illegal and encouraged propaganda that attacked the Catholic religion [C-E]. Did the Protestant hatred of Catholicism here combine with the need to find a common scapegoat, the persecution of whom would help to unite the nation? The Catholic authorities abroad did not always help the situation. The Pope's edict published in 1570 declaring Elizabeth to be excommunicated and releasing her subjects from any allegiance to her was a gift to anyone who wanted to show that all Catholics were traitors to the Queen [F-L]. The plots and murder attempts of a minority of extremists also fed anti-Catholic feeling. A further consideration was the close association of Catholicism with Spain [M], the country that became England's major enemy during Elizabeth's reign.

But Catholicism survived [A-B] and appeared to be stronger in 1600 than in the 1560s or 1570s. Was this due to any change in the character of Catholicism? Some writers have pointed to the importance of the missionary priests who started to arrive in England in 1574 and introduced the spirit of the Counter-Reformation into English Catholicism, giving it a new sense of purpose and the will to resist compromise. More recently the stress has been on the continuity of English Catholicism and the view that the English Catholics were more than just a fading, old-fashioned survival from Mary's reign but had begun to establish a strong identity separate from the established Church even before the missionaries arrived.

Local feeling also had a role to play. There certainly seem to have been Catholic areas [A], but how did these come about? Did they depend on the influence of ex-Marian priests and bishops who remained in the area, the religious loyalties of the local gentry or missionary activity?

## A   Catholic survival

### (i) Report from the Bishop of Peterborough to the Privy Council, 1564

Item, that straggling doctors and priests who have liberty to stray at their pleasures within this realm do much hurt secretly and in corners, therefore it were good that they might be called before the high commissioners and to show their conformity in religion by subscribing or open recantation or else to be restrained from their said liberty . . .

Item, there be divers gentlemen of evil religion that keep schoolmasters in their houses privately, who be of corrupt judgements and do exceeding great hurt as well in those houses where they teach as in the country abroad about them . . .

### (ii) Report from the Bishop of Coventry and Lichfield to the Privy Council, 1564

. . . whereas the country is too much hinderly in all good things pertaining to religion, yet the abiding of Doctor Poole, late bishop of Peterborough, in that shire with Bryan Fowler, Esq, a little from Stafford, causes many people think worse of the regiment and religion than else they would do, because that divers lewd priests have resort thither: but what conference they have, I can not learn.

### (iii) From the Archbishop of Canterbury's visitation of the Chichester diocese, 1569

There is one Father Moses, sometime a friar in Chichester, and he runneth about from one gentleman's house to another with news and letters, being much suspected in religion, and bearing a popish Latin primer with him with Dirge and Litany praying to the saints, and in certain houses he maintained the popish doctrine of Purgatory and praying to dead saints.

## B   Protestant fears

I beseech you to consider what a change there would be if, in the place of the present rulers, those priests, rebels, fugitives and papists, known to be cruel and dissolute and vain, were set at the helm of the church and commonwealth. And if any doubt what a miserable change this would be, let him but remember the late days of Queen Mary, when . . . the pope's authority was wholly restored, and for the continuance thereof a strange nation, proud and insolent, brought into this land to be lords over us. . . . Look, I beseech you, a little back into that time and see what terrible fear all the subjects of this realm – yea, the most forward in popery – were overwhelmed with, both for the doubt they had to live under the yoke of strangers and for the fear they had to lose their abbey-lands.

Sir Walter Mildmay speaking in Parliament, 28 November 1584

## C   Elizabeth appears unaware of danger

Nothing in the world grieveth me more than to see her Majesty believes this increase of papists in her realm can be no danger to her.

The Earl of Leicester, speaking in 1582

## D   Elizabeth's warning to James VI of Scotland

I thank God that you beware so soon of Jesuits, that have been the source of these treacheries in this realm, and will have spread like an evil weed, if at the first they be not weeded out. . . . What religion is this, that they say the way to salvation is to kill the prince for a merit meritorious. This is what they have all confessed without menace or torture. I swear it on my word.

Queen Elizabeth to James VI of Scotland, 15 October 1586

## E   Action in Parliament

Whereas divers persons called or professed Jesuits, seminary priests and other priests, . . . have of late years come and been sent . . . into this realm of England and other the Queen's Majesty's dominions, of purpose (as hath appeared as well by sundry of their own examinations and confessions as by divers other manifest means and proofs) not only to withdraw her Highness' subjects from their due obedience to her Majesty but also to stir up and move sedition, rebellion and open hostility within her Highness' realms and dominions. . . . For reformation whereof be it . . . enacted . . . that all and every Jesuits, seminary priests and other priests whatsoever, made or ordained . . . by any authority . . . from the see of Rome since the feast of the Nativity of St John the Baptist in the first year of her Highness' reign, shall within forty days next after the end of this present session of Parliament depart out of this realm of England and out of all other her Highness' realms and dominions. . . .

And be it further enacted . . . that it shall not be lawful to or for any Jesuit, seminary priest or other such priest, deacon or any religious or ecclesiastical person . . . ordained or professed . . . by any authority . . . from the see of Rome . . . to come into, be or remain in any part of this realm or any other her Highness' dominions after the end of the same forty days . . . and if he do, that then every such offence shall be taken and adjudged to be high treason; and every person so offending shall for his offence be adjudged a traitor, and shall suffer, lose and forfeit as in case of high treason. And every person which . . . shall wittingly and willingly receive, relieve, comfort, aid or maintain any such Jesuit, seminary priest, or other priest, deacon, or religious or ecclesiastical person as is aforesaid, being at liberty or out of hold, knowing him to be a Jesuit, seminary priest or other such priest, deacon, or religious or ecclesiastical person as is aforesaid, shall also for such offence be adjudged a felon without benefit of clergy, and suffer death, lose and forfeit as in case of one attainted of felony.

From the Act Against Jesuits and Seminary Priests, 1585

### F   A secret agent's report

I have revealed the miserable and perfidious design of the enemies of the state, who desire nothing but its total ruin, and to raise and stir up the people of England against their princess by a civil war. This they do by means of evil rumours and defamatory books, popish and contrary to religion, which are transported into England from France at the instance of those who are in flight from their country, and also of the Spanish ambassador and of others who favour them: such as mass-books, other defamatory books written by Jesuits, books of hours and other books serving their purpose. These books are transported from this country to England by the domestic servants of M de Mauvissière, ambassador for the French king there; they import into France from England vestments and furnishings of the popish church which they buy there cheap and sell dear in this country. . . . It is a fact that all the evil and treason which have been discovered have come from giving M de Mauvissière a house beside the River [Thames], to which they are able to carry by night books, letters, packets and all sorts of other things to serve for the ruin of the country. The goods are secretly sold at the ambassador's house by his aforesaid domestic servants, and it is necessary for the good of the country to prevent them from living in that quarter, and in any other regarded as suspect, where they would be able to continue their schemes or wicked enterprises.

Letter to the English ambassador in Paris from one of Sir Francis Walsingham's agents in that city, February 1585

### G   The question of loyalty

I think there can be very few indeed who love their country and religion who do not from their hearts desire to be once more subject to your most clement rule.

Cardinal Allen to Philip II, March 1587

### H   Catholic loyalty to the Queen [written by a Jesuit on the English mission]

It is a point of the Catholic faith . . . that subjects are bound in conscience, under pain of forfeiting their right in Heaven . . . to obey the just laws of their princes; which both the Protestants and Puritans deny with their father Mr Calvin. And therefore if we were not pressed to that which by the general verdict of all ages was judged a breach of the law of God, we should never give your Majesty the least cause of displeasure.

From Robert Southwell: *An Humble Supplication to Her Majestie* (1591 or 1592)

### I The Bloody Question [written by a Jesuit on the English mission describing events during his captivity in 1594]

Another time they had me up for examination with all the other Catholics in our prison in the public place called the Guildhall. Topcliffe was there with many other commissioners; and after they had run through the usual questions and I had given the answers I always gave they came to the point: they wanted, as far as I could see, to find out how we were all disposed towards the government. They hoped to trip us up in the way we spoke about the Queen and then frame a charge against us. Turning to me they asked:

'Do you recognise the Queen as the true and lawful Queen of England?'

'I do,' I answered.

'And in spite of the fact that she has been excommunicated by Pius V,' said Topcliffe.

'I recognise that she is Queen,' I replied, 'though I know too that there has been an excommunication.'

I was aware, of course, the Pope had stated that the excommunication had not yet come into force in England: its application had been withheld until it could be made effective.

Then Topcliffe asked:

'What would you do if the Pope were to send over an army and declare that his only object was to bring the kingdom back to its Catholic allegiance? And if he stated at the same time that there was no other way of re-establishing the Catholic faith; and commanded everyone by his apostolic authority to support him? Whose side would you be on then – the Pope's or the Queen's?'

Then I saw the man's subtlety and wicked cunning. He had so framed his question that whatever I answered I would be sure to suffer for it, either in body or in soul.

I picked the words of my reply.

'I am a loyal Catholic and I am a loyal subject of the Queen. If this were to happen, and I do not think it at all likely, I would behave as a loyal Catholic and as a loyal subject.'

'Oh, no,' he said. 'I want a plain and straight answer. What would you do?'

I answered:

'I have told you what I think and I will not give you any other answer.'
Then he flew into a most violent rage and spat a torrent of oaths at
me . . .

From John Gerard: *The Autobiography of an Elizabethan* (c.1614)

### J Mary, Queen of Scots

. . . Having of long time, to our intolerable grief, seen by how manifold,
most dangerous and execrable practices, Mary . . . commonly called the
Queen of Scots, hath compassed the destruction of your Majesty's
sacred and most royal person . . . and thereby not only to bereave us of
the sincere and true religion of Almighty God . . . but also utterly to
ruinate and overthrow the happy state and commonweal of this realm:
and seeing also what insolent boldness is grown in the heart of the
same queen . . . we cannot find that there is any possible means to
provide for your Majesty's safety, but by the just and speedy execution
of the said queen.

From a petition of Parliament touching Mary, Queen of Scots, 22 November
1586

### K Engraving of Mary, Queen of Scots, published at Antwerp soon after her execution.

**L   A poem about Mary, Queen of Scots, written by a Jesuit**
Alive a Queen, now dead I am a saint;
Once Mary called, my name now Martyr is;
From earthly reign debarred by restraint,
In lieu whereof I reign in heavenly bliss ...
Rue not my death, rejoice at my repose;
It was no death to me but to my woe;
The bud was opened to let out the rose,
The chain was loosed to let the captive go.

From a poem by Robert Southwell, written shortly after Mary's execution

**M   Catholics on stage**
**(i) Henry III comments on the death of the Catholic Duke of Guise**
          ... I swear
I ne'er was King of France until this hour.
This is the traitor that hath spent my gold
In making foreign wars and civil broils.
Did he not draw a sort of English priests
From Douai to the seminary at Rheims,
To hatch forth treason 'gainst their natural queen?
Did he not cause the King of Spain's huge fleet
To threaten England and to menace me?

From Christopher Marlowe: *The Massacre at Paris*, probably published 1600

**(ii) Cardinal Pandulph condemns King John**
Then by the lawful power that I have
Thou shalt stand curs'd and excommunicate;
And blessed shall he be that doth revolt
From his allegiance to an heretic;
And meritorious shall that hand be call'd,
Canonised, and worshipp'd as a saint,
That takes away by any secret course
Thy hateful life.

From William Shakespeare: *King John*, before 1598

# Questions

**1** What do these sources tell us about the nature of English Catholicism
in the years 1559–*c.*1579?                                   **(5 marks)**

**2** What arguments are used in Source B to support legislation against
the Catholics?                                               **(3 marks)**

**3** According to Sources C and D what was Elizabeth's view of the Catholic threat? **(5 marks)**

**4** Read Source H.
   **a** How does Southwell try to stress Catholic loyalty to the Queen? **(2 marks)**
   **b** How does he compare this with the Protestant position? **(2 marks)**
   **c** What, for Elizabeth and her advisers, might be the weak point in his assurances? **(3 marks)**

**5** How useful is Source I for the study of English Catholicism in Elizabeth's reign? **(7 marks)**

**6** Compare Sources J, K and L in their attitude to Mary, Queen of Scots, and account for any differences between them. **(7 marks)**

**7** With reference to Source M, comment on the value of the work of playwrights and poets to the historian of Elizabeth's reign. **(7 marks)**

**8** '... terming themselves Catholics and being indeed spies ... for her Majesty's foreign enemies ... under a false pretext of religion and conscience' (An Act against Popish Recusants, 1593). How far do these sources support this description of English Catholics in the reign of Elizabeth I? **(9 marks)**

# 13 THE ENGLISH BIBLE

'Read Luke 15 (the Prodigal Son) in Tyndale's version of 1526, language which subsequent translators saw no reason to alter by so much as a word, and you may have some understanding of what moved the hearts of English Protestants of the sixteenth and seventeenth centuries.' This was Professor Patrick Collinson's advice in an article published in The Tablet in January 1994.

The vernacular Bible played an important role in the English Reformation. It became the touchstone of reform, one of the characteristics of Protestantism, more so in England than on the continent. Elsewhere in Europe the Catholic Church was already more open to the idea of the Bible in the vernacular and even English Protestants of the sixteenth century acknowledged that foreign Catholics had access to such translations, though they might have a poor opinion of them.

Protestants were eager to have the Bible translated largely due to their growing dependence on the Bible as a source of doctrine and discipline [J]. Without the element of tradition, the handing down of a body of faith by the Church, they turned much more frequently to the Word of God to justify their beliefs and actions. They saw it as their main weapon against the superstition of Rome and the human errors of the papacy. However, the Protestant monopoly on the English Bible did not last and by the end of the century the English Catholics had their own approved translation, either as a result of the demands of Counter-Reformation Catholicism or as a direct challenge to the Protestant versions available [H-I].

What difference did the availability of the English Bible make to the people [K-M]? Erasmus writing about the Scriptures said that he looked forward to the day 'that the husbandman may sing parts of them at his plough, that the weaver may hum them at his shuttle'. But how realistic an ambition was this? How far did this humanist scholar reflect the needs and desires of ordinary people? We have here an example of an attitude that has been noted elsewhere with regard to other aspects of the English Reformation. Perhaps the English Bible was needed by both Protestants and Catholics, but does that mean that there was a widespread demand for it or that it was welcomed wholeheartedly when it arrived?

## A   Resistance to a vernacular Bible

No one henceforth shall translate any text of Holy Scripture into the English language on his own authority, by way of book, booklet or tract ... under pain of the greater excommunication, until it shall have been approved by the diocesan of the place, or, if the occasion demands it, by the provincial council.

From the Constitutions of Archbishop Arundel against the Lollards, 1409

## B   Fear of adulteration

Many children of iniquity, maintainers of Luther's sect, blinded through extreme wickedness, wandering from the way of truth and the Catholic faith, have craftily translated the New Testament into our English tongue, intermeddling therewith many heretical articles and erroneous opinions, seducing the common people, attempting by their wicked and perverse interpretations to profane the majesty of the scriptures, which hitherto have remained undefiled, and craftily to abase the most holy word of God, and the true sense of the same, of the which translation there are many books printed, some with glosses, and some without, containing in the English tongue that pestiferous and most pernicious poison dispersed in all our diocese of London.

Cuthbert Tunstall, Bishop of London, to his archdeacons, 24 October 1526

## C   Royal Patronage: Anne Boleyn described by her chaplain

To the right high, mighty, and most excellent princess Elizabeth, by the grace of God queen of England, France and Ireland, Defender of the Faith etc ...

And that [her maids of honour] should not consume the [time] in vain toys and poetical fancies as in elder time they wonted were, she caused a desk in her chamber upon the which she commanded an English Bible to be laid, whereunto every person might have recourse to read upon when they would. ... Neither did her majesty disdain in her own person sundry times to repair to the common desk where the said Bible was placed, yielding herein example to others to the like endeavour.

From William Latymer: *A brief treatise or chronicle of the most virtuous lady Anne Boleyn late Queen of England*

## D  Anne Boleyn's copy of Tyndale's translation of the New Testament

## E  Royal Patronage: Queen Elizabeth and the Bible

For when her grace had learned that the Bible in English should there be
offered, she thanked the City therefore, promised the reading thereof
most diligently, and incontinent commanded that it should be brought.
At the receipt whereof, how reverently did she with both her hands take
it, kiss it, and lay it upon her breast to the great comfort of the lookers
on.

From Richard Tottel: *The Quenes maiesties passage through the citie of
London to Westminster the day before her coronation* (1559)

## F  Cranmer's preface to the Great Bible

Wherefore, in a few words to comprehend the largeness and utility of
the scripture, how it contains fruitful instruction and erudition for every
man; if any things be necessary to be learned, of the holy scripture we
may learn it. . . . Here may all manner of persons . . . learn all things what
they ought to believe, what they ought to do, and what they should not
do, as well concerning Almighty God, as also concerning themselves
and all other. Briefly, to the reading of scripture none can be the enemy,

but that either [they] be so sick that they love not to hear of any medicine, or else that they be so ignorant that they know not scripture to be the most healthful medicine.

... There is nothing so good in this world, but it may be abused, and turned from fruitful and wholesome to hurtful and noisome. ... Wherefore I would advise you all, that cometh to the reading or hearing of this book, which is the word of God, the most precious jewel and holy relic that remaineth upon earth, that ye bring with you the fear of God, and that ye do it with all due reverence, and use your knowledge thereof, not to vain-glory of frivolous disputation, but to the honour of God, increase of virtue, and edification both of yourselves and other ...

From Thomas Cranmer's Preface to the Great Bible, 1540

### G   The Bible in Henry VIII's reign
Recourse must be had to the Catholic and Apostolic Church for the decision of controversies; and therefore all books of the Old and New Testaments in English, being of Tyndal's false translation, or comprising any matter of Christian religion, articles of the faith, or Holy Scripture, contrary to the doctrine set forth since Anno Dom. 1540 or to be set forth by the king, shall be abolished. ... No person shall retain any English books or writings concerning matter against the holy and blessed sacrament of the altar, or for the maintenance of anabaptists, or other books abolished by the king's proclamation. There shall be no annotations or preambles in Bibles or New Testaments in English. The Bible shall not be read in English in any church. No women or artificers, prentices, journeymen, serving men of the degree of yeomen or under, husbandmen, nor labourers, shall read the New Testament in English.

From the Act for the Advancement of True Religion, 1543

### H   Catholics and the English Bible
On Monday 16th December, the New Testament was divided up so that it could be translated into English. ...

On Friday 20th December, the prolocutor ... presented a document listing certain words requiring careful consideration in the translation of the New Testament, and their interpretation was discussed.

From the record of Cardinal Pole's legatine synod held at Westminster, 1555–56

### I   The desire for a Catholic translation
When the priests are preaching to the unlearned and are obliged on the

spur of the moment to translate some passage which they have quoted into the vulgar tongue, they often do it inaccurately and with unpleasant hesitation, because either there is no vernacular version of the words or it does not then and there occur to them. Our adversaries on the other hand have at their fingers' ends from some heretical version, all those passages of Scripture which seem to make for them, and by a certain deceptive adaptation and alteration of the sacred words produce the effect of appearing to say nothing but what comes from the Bible. This evil might be remedied if we too had some Catholic version of the Bible, for all the English versions are most corrupt. . . .

Perhaps indeed it would have been more desirable that the Scripture had never been translated into barbarous tongues: nevertheless at the present day when, either from heresy or other causes, the curiosity of men, even of those who are not bad, is so great, and there is often also such need of reading the Scriptures in order to confute our opponents, it is better that there should be a faithful and Catholic translation than that men should use a corrupt version to their peril or destruction: the more so since the dangers which arise from reading certain more difficult passages may be obviated by suitable notes.

From a letter from Cardinal William Allen, *c.*1578

**J  A Protestant view of the Bible – an illustration from the 1576 edition of Foxe's *Book of Martyrs***

### K   Protestant zeal in the 1520s

The fervent zeal of those Christian days seemed much superior to these our days and times, as manifestly may appear by their sitting up all night in reading and hearing: also by their expenses and charges in buying of books in English, of whom some gave five marks, some more, some less, for a book; some gave a load of hay for a few chapters of St James or of St Paul in English.

From John Foxe: *Acts and Monuments (Book of Martyrs)* (1563)

### L   The provision of the Bible in the parishes

Where, by injunctions heretofore set forth by the authority of the King's royal majesty . . . it was ordained and commanded amongst other things that in all and singular parish churches there should be provided by a certain day, now expired, at the costs of the curates and parishioners, Bibles containing the Old and New Testament in the English tongue, to be fixed and set up openly in every of the said parish churches . . . his majesty is informed that divers and many towns and parishes within this his realm have negligently omitted their duties in the accomplishment thereof; whereof his highness marveleth not a little. And . . . doth straightly charge and command that . . . every town and parish . . . not having already Bibles provided within their parish churches, shall on this side the Feast of All Saints next coming, buy and provide Bibles of the largest and greatest volume, and cause the same to be set and fixed in every of the said parish churches.

From a Royal Proclamation of the 6 May, 1541

### M   The vernacular Bible available, but little read

The most sacred and holy Bible, I say, is now had among us in our vulgar tongue, and freely permitted to be read of all men universally, at times convenient, without any let or perturbation, even in the churches: but how many read it? Verily a man may come into some churches and see the Bible so enclosed and wrapped about with dust, even as the pulpit in like manner is both with dust and cobwebs, that with his finger he may write upon the Bible this epitaph: *ecce nunc in pulvere dormio*, that is to say, 'Behold I sleep now in the dust'. So little pleasure have these filthy swine and currish dogs in that most sweet and singular treasure.

From Thomas Becon: *The News Out of Heaven* (1560)

# Questions

**1** Using your own knowledge, indicate how Source A helps to explain the views in Source B. **(4 marks)**

**2** Assess the reliability of Latymer's account in Source C. Refer to Sources D and E in your answer. **(6 marks)**

**3** According to Sources F and G, what problems might arise from the publication of an English Bible? **(4 marks)**

**4** What evidence is there in the sources for a change in the Catholic attitude towards an English Bible? **(5 marks)**

**5** Analyse the way in which Source J uses pictorial images to present its view of the English Bible. **(6 marks)**

**6** Compare the value of Sources K, L and M as evidence of popular reactions to the English Bible. **(7 marks)**

**7** To what extent do these sources show that the Bible in English was an essential element in the Protestant Reformation. **(8 marks)**

# 14 HISTORIOGRAPHY: THE REIGN OF QUEEN MARY

Textbooks, teachers and examiners proudly present students with sources or different views from historians and, as if they were doing them a favour, tell them to make up their own minds on the basis of the evidence. And at some point many students will simply throw up their hands or throw down their pens and ask just once for a simple answer to 'What really happened?' When all historians start to agree in their interpretations of the past the student's life will indeed be easier but the study of history will lose much of its fascination.

Mary's reign provides rich potential for dispute. The subsequent religious history of the country seemed to mark out her reign as an aberration and it also fell victim to the anti-Catholicism that came to be a characteristic of many Englishmen. The reign was judged in the context of the historian's own era rather than in the context of the 1550s. The events of the reign were such as to make an objective judgement difficult. How, for example, do we view the killing of so many Protestants?

Why do interpretations differ? What causes people to challenge the existing views on a topic? Sometimes it may be new evidence or new techniques. Sometimes old evidence is looked at in a new way. In the study of the English Reformation there is the potential of religious belief to nudge at an historian's opinions. Would it help or hinder the student to know, for example, that Eamon Duffy is a practising Catholic who writes frequently for the Catholic press or that Derek Wilson was an Anglican lay reader?

A    The frontispiece of John Foxe: *Acts and Monuments (Book of Martyrs)* (1563) [Protestants are shown on the left and Catholics are shown on the right; Christ sits in judgement at the top]

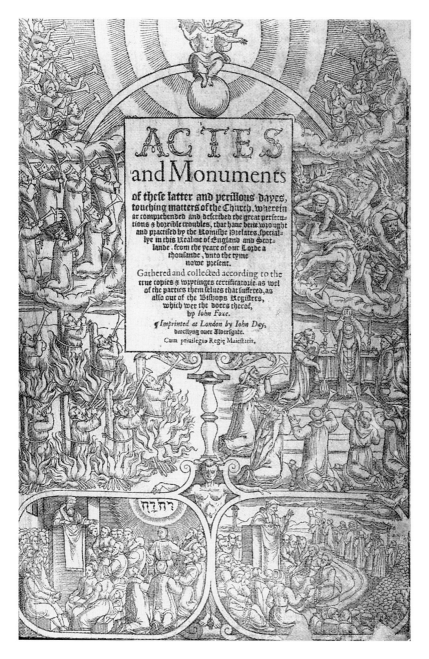

## B The nature of Mary's policy

It should have been engraven on Mary's heart, not that she lost Calais but that she failed to discover the Counter-Reformation. Her government was haunted by the ghost of her father; intent upon the legal undoing of his legalism it forgot that in the last resort religious teaching mattered infinitely more than ecclesiastical legislation. The apparent ['exceptional' in 1st edition, 1964] religious and cultural sterility of these years has often been observed. For creative instruction the ceaseless processions made by government order around the streets and churches of London provided a poor substitute.

From A.G. Dickens: *The English Reformation* (2nd edition, 1989)

## C English Counter-Reformation?

Indeed, the religious priorities in evidence in the attempts to re-establish Catholic belief and practice in Mary's reign closely parallel much that is often thought to be most characteristic of the Counter-Reformation. The leaders of the Marian church did in fact possess a realistic set of objectives, based on a shrewd and fundamentally sound assessment of the impact of reform on the broad mass of the population. Far from pursuing a programme of blind reaction, the Marian authorities consistently sought to promote a version of traditional Catholicism which had absorbed whatever they saw as positive in the Edwardine and Henrician reforms, and which were subtly but distinctively different from the Catholicism of the 1520s.... There is, moreover, considerable evidence that the religious programme of the Marian church was widely accepted, and was establishing itself in the parishes ...

Those who have criticised the Marian regime's use of the printing press have neglected one aspect of the publishing history of the reign which is crucial to any adequate understanding of the religious programme of the Marian church. Thirty-five editions of the Sarum primer survive from Mary's reign, and four of the York primer.... This rate of production swamps that of any earlier period ... their character and content disposes decisively of any idea that religion was merely reactionary or represented an unreflecting return to the pattern which had prevailed before the break with Rome.

From Eamon Duffy: *The Stripping of the Altars* (1992)

## D What were Mary's chances of success?

John Strype in the seventeenth century, James Froude in the nineteenth, and to a lesser extent A.F. Pollard all echoed Foxe's judgement, and concluded that Mary had failed because she sought to drive her people in a direction contrary to that which destiny had mapped out for them. Such determinism does not appeal today, and the emphasis of recent scholarship has been rather on the achievements of her reign – the sound administration, sensible financial policies and practical approach to ecclesiastical reconstruction. . . . Today, the main question which is asked about Mary and her reign is whether they would have succeeded, given more time. In other words, whether Mary really misjudged her subjects in any fundamental way. . . .

Finally, there was the question of heresy. Persecution neither stamped out nor silenced the Protestants during the three and a half years in which it was applied. The political tone of the Protestant leadership changed significantly as the older generation of leaders went to the flames. The non-resistance principles of Cranmer and Latimer were, by 1556, being replaced by the revolutionary theories of Knox, Goodman and Ponet. The development of a martyrology, and the appearance of a new generation or radical leaders, many of them without commitment to the royal supremacy, increased the danger of Protestant insurrection. A situation similar to that in France or the Netherlands could easily have emerged in the 1560s. We simply do not know what would have happened if Mary had lived longer, but it should not be assumed that the government of Philip and Mary would have continued to function with increasing stability and success.

From David Loades: *Mary Tudor* (1989)

### E Was Mary's reign an aberration?

Historians have often regarded Mary's reign as an aberration, an inconvenient disruption of the natural process of Reformation. . . . Mary's Catholic regime was seeking to dam the tide of history, and it had to fail: doomed from the beginning and disintegrating at the end. . . . The inexorable forces of modernisation which had been generated under Henry and strengthened under Edward were tested under Mary, and they triumphed under Elizabeth. Or so it may seem. But we have already seen that the demand for religious change had been weak, and loyalty to the old ways was not destroyed by political diktat; the Protestants had become a significant minority movement, but they had not broken through to mass support. From the perspective of 1558 (if not of 1559), it is the reign of Edward which appears an aberration, disrupting the process of Catholic restoration which had begun in 1538 and was to continue under Mary.

The Marian reconstruction of Catholicism was a success. It was not a total success, for the Protestants could not all be crushed and the indifferent could not all be made enthusiasts – at least, not in five years. But the evidence from the parishes is of considerable and continuing support for traditional services and celebrations, and Pole was leading a promising reform programme which tackled the structural problems of the English Church. The physical consequences of two political Reformations had been repaired as far as political and economic realities allowed, and expenditure on churches was high. In Mary's last year recruitment to the priesthood was better than it had been for thirty years, and the laity's giving to parish religion was probably greater than for twenty. In England, religious division may have been easing; the persecution had slackened, as determination among both heretics and hunters apparently declined. Abroad, Protestant exiles were in dispute and despair; in 1558 their printed propaganda declined in volume and increased in hysteria, advocating overthrow of Mary before the restoration of Catholicism became irreversible. . . . And then Mary made her only serious – her fatal – error: she died on 17 November 1558.

From Christopher Haigh: *English Reformations* (1993)

### F 'A Bad Thing'
. . . while [Edward] was sitting on the throne everyone in the land was forced to become Protestant, so that Broody Mary would be able to put them to death afterwards for not being Roman Catholics. A good many people protested against this treatment and thus it was proved that they were Protestants, but most of the people decanted and were all right. Broody Mary's reign was, however, a Bad Thing, since England is bound to be C. of E., so all the executions were wasted.

From W.C. Sellar and R.J. Yeatman: *1066 and All That* (1930)

### G Off the fence
The burnings began in February, 1555. A neurotic queen, deserted by her husband, angry at the sullen hostility of her people, convinced of the holiness of her cause and egged on by Spanish priests familiar with the methods of the Inquisition, personally urged the bishops to proceed to the 'final solution' of the heresy problem. . . . If we said that two thousand people endured considerable suffering for their faith during the reign of Mary Tudor we should be taking a very conservative figure. It is a number that can leave us in no doubt as to the impact which the English Bible and the unfettered preaching of the word of God had made upon the nation. No other cause in Britain's history has been ennobled by the sufferings of so many heroes and heroines. If there was any doubt about the religious road England was destined to take at the beginning of Mary's reign, there was none by the end of it. The blood of the martyrs ensured that England would remain a Protestant country and that Catholicism would, for centuries, be the religion of a downtrodden minority.

From Derek Wilson: *The People and the Book. The Revolutionary Impact of the English Bible 1380–1611* (1976)

# Questions

**1** Use Source A to show how John Foxe contributed to later interpretations of Mary's reign. **(4 marks)**

**2** What reason can you suggest for Dickens changing the wording in Source B? **(3 marks)**

**3** To what extent is Source F of value as evidence for views on Mary's reign? **(4 marks)**

**4** Comment on the objectivity of Source G. **(5 marks)**

**5** To what extent do you agree with the view that 'In dealing with Mary I's reign it is difficult to avoid anachronistic sympathies'? **(5 marks)**

**6** With reference to the Reformation, examine the extent to which an historian's religious allegiance will have an influence on his or her work? **(6 marks)**

**7** Use these sources to produce (a) an argument in favour of Mary's policies, and (b) an argument against Mary's policies. **(10 marks)**

# DEALING WITH EXAMINATION QUESTIONS

## Specimen Answers to Source-based Questions

Questions based on Chapter 2 – Henry VIII's Reformation (see pages 11–19).

## Questions

**1 a** According to Source A, what problem faced the English Church in the mid-1530s? **(2 marks)**

**b** How is the second item in Source A relevant to the annulment of Henry VIII's marriage to Catherine of Aragon? **(2 marks)**

**2** How useful are Sources F and G in showing how serious a problem heresy was in the reign of Henry VIII? **(6 marks)**

**3 a** In what ways does Source E 'tighten up' the doctrine of the Eucharist expressed in Source B? **(2 marks)**

**b** Why would Anne Askew's argument on the Eucharist in Source H not have convinced her accusers? **(3 marks)**

**4 a** How does Source I reflect the attitude of John Bale to Anne Askew and her beliefs? **(5 marks)**

**b** Comment on John Bale's use of language in Source H. **(4 marks)**

**5** Comment on the significance of the letters in Sources J and K. **(6 marks)**

**6** 'Henry died a Catholic, though a rather bad Catholic' (Haig). To what extent do these sources support such an assessment of Henry VIII?
**(8 marks)**

## Points to Note About These Questions

**1 a** This is a 'comprehension' question to show that you have understood the content of Source A. Paraphrase the relevant parts of the source rather than simply copying them.

**b** Understanding of the extract is here combined with your own knowledge of the marriage problem.

**2** The sources should be considered in terms of both content and context. Does the content actually tell us anything about the heresy problem e.g. its extent, the form it took, who was involved? The context of the sources –

who wrote them and why – will also affect your judgement of how useful they might be. Even if the question does not specifically ask about the reliability of a source it is still likely that you will have to comment on it in an assessment of its utility.

**3 a** This requires a careful reading of the source and a clear understanding of the doctrine of the Eucharist.

**b** First you need to identify Askew's argument and then match it to the likely beliefs of her accusers.

**4 a** Some knowledge of the symbols used in religious art is helpful with this question but a good attempt could be made by picking up on the significance of the Bible and Bible quotation and relating these to some of Bale's comments.

**b** This is simply a question of showing how Bale's choice of words and phrases reflects his views on Anne Askew and her accusers. Avoid lengthy quotations but do refer to individual words and phrases.

**5** This question is on the significance of two particular letters not letters in general. When two sources are paired in this way without the words 'compare' or 'contrast', then the main significance is likely to be something that they have in common.

**6** The quotation could easily be used as part of an essay title. Be sure to keep to the sources in presenting your argument since an excellent essay that ignores the sources cannot gain marks. 'To what extent . . .' could result in three possible responses: (a) They totally support the statement; (b) they do not support the statement; (c) they seem to do both (a) and (b), in which case you need to balance the two arguments. A conclusion is important in this kind of question.

# Specimen Answers

**1 a** According to Source A, what problem faced the English Church in the mid-1530s? **(2 marks)**

Source A indicates that too many different religious opinions have become current in England and that they are provoking too much argument. Some people are putting forward Protestant ideas, for example priests having wives, while others are defending traditional practices.

**1 b** How is the second item in Source A relevant to the annulment of Henry VIII's marriage to Catherine of Aragon? **(2 marks)**

The source refers to no man being able to change God's law. Henry maintained that his marriage to Catherine was forbidden by God's law, as expressed in the Book of Leviticus, and that the Pope did not have the authority to set this law aside. Hence his papal dispensation to marry Catherine had been worthless.

**2** How useful are Sources F and G in showing how serious a problem heresy was in the reign of Henry VIII? **(6 marks)**

In 1539 the Act of Six Articles had settled a Catholic doctrine on Henry's English Church but both Sources F and G indicate that this did not mean an end to religious dissent and that heresy continued to pose a problem. Although Hilles mentions a pardon for 'all heresies' he goes on to give details of a number of exceptions that seem to show that Henry considered heresy an important issue at the time. It appears from this source that the religious changes had thrown up a large number of Protestants who wanted further reform in the Church and this is supported by the proclamation in G. In this proclamation Henry declares that people have taken advantage of the situation to spread unofficial translations of the Bible and heretical books.

Hilles indicates another problem. Henry also had to deal with those who denied his supremacy. Hilles implies that when dealing with the Catholic opposition, Henry also needed to act against the Protestants in order to reassure his subjects of his own orthodoxy in doctrine. From this it might be inferred that heresy was not necessarily a major problem in itself but that Henry needed to be seen to be doing something about it. However, the issuing of the proclamation five years later does reinforce the idea that Henry saw heresy as a genuine problem and a threat to unity in his kingdom.

The utility of these sources lies in the information they provide on the attention given to the heresy problem and also the possible reasons for action being taken. The nature of the sources should also be considered. Hilles admits that he can only speculate on the reasons for the execution of the Protestants. Although, as a Protestant, he had a real interest in what happened, he was writing as a private individual and his perception of heresy would not have matched that of the religious authorities. The proclamation on the other hand does seem to show that heresy was strong enough to prompt royal action.

**3 a** In what way does Source E 'tighten up' the doctrine of the Eucharist expressed in Source B? **(2 marks)**

Although source B accepts the doctrine of the real presence in the Eucharist, it leaves open the possibility of the substance of the bread and wine remaining in the sacrament. However, the Six Articles emphasises transubstantiation and that no substance of bread and wine remains in the sacrament.

**3 b** Why would Anne Askew's argument on the Eucharist in Source H not have convinced her accusers? **(3 marks)**

Anne Askew draws attention to the bread turning mouldy; that is, showing the physical qualities of bread. However, her accusers would have maintained the Catholic doctrine that, although the substance of the bread changed at the words of consecration, the accidents, or physical qualities, remained the same.

**4 a** How does Source I reflect the attitude of John Bale to Anne Askew and her beliefs? **(5 marks)**

Anne Askew is shown holding the palm traditionally associated with Christian martyrs, a reference to her dying for the faith. The beast at her feet wears the triple crown of the Pope and represents her rejection of and spiritual victory over Catholicism. She holds a Bible. This and the quotation from Psalm 116 to the left of the picture show her dependence on the Bible. This is also borne out by Source H where she expresses her preference for Bible reading to attending mass and Bale commends her attitude, saying that since the mass is not to be found in the Bible then it did not belong to the true faith.

**4 b** Comment on John Bale's use of language in Source H. **(4 marks)**

Bale's language leaves the reader in no doubt as to his loyalties. Askew's interrogator is not merely condemned as crafty but is associated with the antichrist while Askew herself is presented as an 'innocent lamb', an image that for many would have prompted thoughts of Christ himself, the Lamb of God sacrificed by his opponents. The parallel is strengthened by a comparison between Askew's trial and the trial of Christ. The reference to 'wicked Pharisees' shows clearly his view of Askew's opponents. The use of such strong language obviously indicates that this is not going to be an objective account of proceedings.

**5** Comment on the significance of the letters in Sources J and K.

**(6 marks)**

In Source J Cranmer writes that people may have been deceived by Anne Boleyn, who gave the appearance of being a sincere supporter of reform in the Church, loving both 'God and his gospel'. His great worry in this extract seems to be that, in rejecting Anne, Henry will also reject the religious policy that was associated with her. Although Cranmer refers to Henry's own 'zeal unto the truth' the letter clearly indicates that he felt Anne had been a very strong influence on Henry in religious matters. A similar role is envisaged for Anne of Cleves in Source K. Here, John Butler is quite explicit that he feels the influence of the new queen will help the spread of the reformed faith in England.

Both these letters indicate the importance attached to individuals in attendance on the king. They seem to show that some at least of his contemporaries felt that Henry could be pushed in one direction or another by those around him. However, Cranmer may have been thinking mainly of the link between the Boleyn marriage and the break from Rome, rather than any genuine religious influence wielded by Anne, and fearing that her execution might clear the way to a reconciliation with the Pope. As for John Butler, he, or his English correspondents, may simply have been indulging in wishful thinking.

6 'Henry died a Catholic, though a rather bad Catholic' (Haig). To what extent do these sources support such an assessment of Henry VIII?

**(8 marks)**

The Ten Articles of 1536 have often been read through Protestant spectacles but these extracts at least show a fairly orthodox approach to doctrine and religious practices. The discussion of justification does indicate that it is not 'faith alone' that justifies but a combination of faith and good works and this view is represented also in Source D where Henry altered the wording of the Bishops' Book in a way that totally changed its meaning and brought it into line with his more Catholic belief. Source C shows that Henry had not in fact read the original version carefully. On the question of images, prayers to the saints and the Church's traditional practices, the Ten Articles do not condemn them but rather praise them as long as their true meaning and limitations are understood. On the Eucharist the Ten Articles are ambiguous rather than positively Catholic or Protestant.

It was this ambiguity that the Six Articles were meant to tackle and the extract quoted sets out explicitly the Catholic doctrine of transubstantiation. Henry's Catholic orthodoxy is also shown in his dealings with heretics. The order to preachers in Source A had already referred to the possibilities of religious dissent and this was tackled in the proclamation of 1546. The action against heretics described by Richard Hilles was motivated partly by a need to conciliate conservative elements in the country but can also be explained by Henry's genuine desire to retain some degree of Catholic orthodoxy as demonstrated in the other sources. Hilles, as a disappointed reformer, might have found it difficult to understand why 'preachers of the gospel' should have to be executed. However, another reformer, John Bale, had no doubts in this matter and identified the Henrician regime that executed Anne Askew with a Catholicism that depended on the Pope.

However, at about the same time that Anne Askew was being tried and convicted, Henry, if we are to believe the accounts by John Foxe in Sources L and M, was planning to move away from his traditional position. As a convinced Protestant, Foxe might be regarded as too biased a source. However he had access to material from members of Cranmer's household and the two stories, with their references to 'pulling down of roods and suppressing the ringing of bells' are internally consistent. If they can be accepted, then Henry planned a religious change that can in no way be described as Catholic and which he was only prevented by death from implementing. Source L also indicates another motive that could explain this new radicalism and that is the influence of foreign policy on his religious policy. If it curbed further change in the story in L then perhaps it also explains his apparent volte-face in M.

These changes were never put into effect but it does not free Henry from the charge of being a 'bad Catholic'. A consistent element in these sources is Henry's rejection of papal authority. This is implied in the second item of

Source A, and in Source F he executes those who deny his supremacy along with the Protestant heretics. It is as Supreme Head that he sanctioned the Ten Articles and also gave his approval to the Bishops' Book. It is Henry's book of doctrine that is the touchstone of orthodoxy in the proclamation of 1546.

Ignoring the question of supremacy, Henry, according to these sources, is Catholic in his public utterances and in the religion that he implements in England. However, Sources L and M particularly seem to challenge the sincerity of his Catholicism and imply either that he grew more radical with age or that he was prepared to sacrifice religion to the demands of foreign policy. If one also accepts papal supremacy as an element of Catholicism then these sources certainly show him to be a 'bad Catholic'.

# *Preparing Essay Answers*

Essays still form the major part of the written work produced in most History courses and of most A-level and Higher level examinations. Even in source-based questions some of the responses approach being essays in both style and length and some of the following hints can be applied to them as well as to essays:

1  Examiners are not trying to trick you with their questions. Check carefully the wording of the essay title and then do what it asks you. In particular this means looking for the key words, for example 'Why . . . ?', 'To what extent . . . ?'.

2  Having checked the meaning of the title, make sure that your essay is relevant to that title. If dates are included in the title, do not go outside those dates – you cannot be credited for such material. Dates are normally carefully chosen so think again before restricting yourself to too limited a period within the dates set. Keep asking yourself: 'Is this relevant?', 'Is this significant?'

3  Do not reproduce your standard essay on a topic. Examiners want the answer to the question they asked, not the question you think they should have asked. Resign yourself to the fact that some of your best work will never be reproduced for a public examination.

4  Do plan your essay and try to stick to that plan. Changing your mind halfway through an essay or writing a conclusion at odds with the argument put forward in the main body of the essay are not quite the same thing as weighing up the two sides of an argument.

5  Be organised in your writing. You cannot go far wrong with a short introductory paragraph that defines any terms that might require definition and sets out the main points to be discussed; follow this with a series of paragraphs discussing these points in turn and finish off with a concluding paragraph which brings together in a brief summary all you have just written and relates it clearly to the title. Do not make your paragraphs too long.

6  Support everything you say. Any argument will need evidence to back it up. That is why it is necessary to have a good knowledge of the material before attempting an essay.

7  Write clearly and do not use words and phrases if you are in any way unsure about their meaning. Keep to simple, direct English.

8  Finally, there is nothing here that your teachers could not tell you. Do pay attention to what they say about and write on your essays. Sometimes these comments will be of more use to you than the essay itself.

# *Possible Essay Titles*

**1**  How adequately did the pre-Reformation Church in England meet the religious needs of the country?

There will need to be some discussion of what is meant by 'religious needs' which may not be as straightforward as it sounds. Some students may have their own idea of religious needs but should not presume that these were shared by the people of the sixteenth century. They should also recognise the different views held at the time. Did the demands of the reformers reflect the needs of the majority? Historians such as Scarisbrick and Duffy are very useful here and examiners could expect candidates to show some awareness of their work. There should be some acknowledgement that there was room for improvement and reference made to both 'Protestant' reformers and critics from within the Church. Areas covered could include parish life, the religious orders, the bishops and the real or potential abuses such as non-residence and pluralism.

**2**  To what extent was the Henrician Reformation the result of the King's marriage problem?

This should be a fairly straightforward essay as long as the first words are not ignored. Deal first with the marriage problem and the role it had in setting a train of events in motion and then go on to look at the other factors that contributed to the Henrician Reformation – for example, a general need or desire for reform, the influence of a group of genuine reformers (Cranmer, Cromwell), the development of Henry's ambitions as he became more aware of the possibilities open to him. The conclusion could then consider all these points together and produce a final judgement on the importance of each one, particularly in relation to the marriage problem. Finally, note that it is the Henrician Reformation – do not go beyond Henry's reign.

**3**  Compare the content and context of the Ten Articles of 1536 and the Six Articles of 1539. What do they reveal about the Henrician Reformation?

This is not an essay to attempt without a very clear idea of what these two sets of articles say. The initial comparison should be relatively simple, but be careful with the Ten Articles because it is easy to overplay their Protestant character. The context should deal with why the articles were produced and the influences on them, which could be political and personal as well as religious. The second part of the title indicates the kind of comments required in dealing with the content and context. For example, what do they show of the methods and motives of the Henrician Reformation?

**4** What factors influenced the religious policies of the years 1532–47?

Obviously this essay requires a good knowledge of the details of religious policy during these years, but that is only the starting point. A chronological treatment would be acceptable but it should not become simply a list of religious changes. The emphasis is on *why* the policy developed in the way that it did. Each change must be seen to have a reason. Alternatively the essay might be organised by 'factors' such as the demands of foreign policy, fear of heresy, pressure from individuals or factions, popular pressure, Henry's own beliefs. Each factor should be illustrated with examples.

**5** The Pilgrimage of Grace was 'a protest on behalf of the old religion'. How true is this statement?

The Pilgrimage of Grace was a major event and examiners can expect students to know it well. A knowledge of the actual demands made by the pilgrims and of the kind of people who took part is needed for this essay. The title focuses on the religious element but students should also be able to comment on economic, social and political factors. For example, Elton's work on the links with court factions could be discussed.

**6** To what extent was England still a Catholic country in 1547?

A successful essay must provide a clear idea of what Catholic means in this context. The question can be answered on two levels. First did the official position fit the description 'Catholic'? Reference should be made to the supremacy, the end of the religious orders, statements on doctrine and on religious practices. This could lead on to an assessment of how far the changes had been accepted by the population as a whole. Did the official position reflect the beliefs of the people?

**7** What were the consequences of the dissolution of the monasteries?

This should be a discussion of both short-term and long-term consequences. The first part should deal with immediate reactions such as the Pilgrimage of Grace, the effect the dissolution had on local communities and the fate of the monasteries themselves – the monks and nuns, the libraries and treasures. The redistribution of land was a major long-term consequence, giving many of the land-owning classes a vested interest in at least one aspect of the Reformation. The effect on the membership of the House of Lords and its implications could be considered.

**8** Did the English Reformation owe more to Thomas Cromwell or to Thomas Cranmer?

It would not be easy to provide a continuous comparison of these individuals and the essay is more likely to divide into a Cromwell section and a Cranmer section. There is nothing wrong with this but try to insert references to the other individual at intervals if only as a reminder of the theme of the essay. Note that it is the English Reformation not just the Henrician Reformation. Do not put Cromwell automatically into second place simply because his career was confined to Henry VIII's reign. Consider the possible long-term implications of his actions and his patronage of reformers. The conclusion must be in the form of a direct comparison between the two.

**9** Why did Somerset and Northumberland encourage the Protestant reformation and what were the results of their actions?

This is not just a version of the 'Good Somerset versus Bad Northumberland' essay, although it may well include comparative judgements of the two of them. The essay could fall into two main parts – reasons followed by results. Treatment of the two dukes should include an assessment of their religious commitment as well as motives of greed, ambition and politics. 'Results' refers most obviously to the actual religious regime that they tried to enforce but the popular attitude to Protestantism should also be considered. These attitudes could have been affected by how the people interpreted the two dukes' motives.

**10** How Protestant was England by 1553?

This requires a good understanding of the religious issues and just what practices and beliefs can be regarded as Protestant. A simple description of the official situation should be the starting point. The essay should then go on to deal with people's reactions to the official policy and consider how far Protestantism had been accepted by the country as a whole. Examples of resistance should be included. The date in the title does not rule out a reference to the beginning of Mary's reign if it can be used to illustrate attitudes in Edward's reign.

**11** To what extent was Mary I successful in restoring Catholicism to England?

This essay should start by indicating what Mary aimed to restore. Did she aim to recreate the Catholicism of the 1520s or were there going to be differences in emphasis? What limitations to the restoration were imposed on her? The monasteries would provide a good case study. The reaction of the people must be considered and the extent to which they accepted Mary's Catholicism. Comment on the lack of time and a successor.

**12** How far can the Elizabethan religious settlement be regarded as the product of Elizabeth's own religious opinions?

See specimen answer on page 125.

**13** Why were the Puritans unsuccessful in making any changes to the religious settlement of 1559?

The essay should indicate the changes that the Puritans wanted and make clear that there were many different demands from the moderate to the extreme. The key element in blocking any change was the Queen herself and there should be a full treatment of why she disliked Puritanism. Consider also changes during the reign. The nature of the demands affected the nature of the response and moderates failed in their aims because of their association with extremists, who became more vocal as the years went by without their making any progress. There was also a growing number of people who had known no other system than the settlement.

**14** Why were the Puritans dissatisfied with the Elizabethan Church?

This question requires a sound knowledge of Puritan demands from dissatisfaction with aspects of the liturgy to attacks on the episcopal system. Balance this with a description of how the established church disappointed them. Many had originally hoped that the 1559 settlement was a stopgap and were disappointed by Elizabeth's refusal to change it. Look also at the actions of some of the bishops in suppressing Puritans. Other aspects could include poorly-paid clergy and too great an involvement with the secular world.

**15** Did the Catholics or the Puritans pose the greater threat to the Elizabethan religious settlement?

The two groups are probably best dealt with one after the other and then compared directly in a conclusion, although it might be possible to provide a parallel treatment. Take into account changes during Elizabeth's reign. Did the Catholicism of the 1560s and 1570s pose the same threat as that of the 1580s and 1590s? Consider the different kinds of Puritan. There were those who wanted to modify the settlement and those who wanted almost to overthrow it. Foreign links are important and it is worth remembering that no Puritan attempted to assassinate Elizabeth.

**16** To what extent were the missionary priests responsible for the preservation of English Catholicism during the reign of Elizabeth?

This presents an opportunity to refer to the work of Dickens or Bossey, who stress the role of the missionary priests, and Haigh and Scarisbrick, who give the survivors from Mary's reign some credit. The most common weakness in answering this question is likely to be a lack of knowledge of the nature of the Catholic survival in the early years of the reign. Treatment of these years is essential to put the later work of the missionary priests in context, whether to enhance their achievement or not.

**17** How significant are foreign affairs in the study of Catholicism and Puritanism in the reign of Elizabeth I?

There could be two aspects to this essay. First the direct link between these two groups and their co-religionists or sympathisers on the continent could be considered. How did Catholicism benefit from its foreign contacts and what support did Puritans get from continental reformers? The second aspect is the way attitudes to Catholics and Puritans varied according to England's relations with other countries. For example, how did war with Spain affect the position of English Catholics?

**18**  How important was the role of the monarch in the religious changes of the sixteenth century?

A chronological treatment with a concluding summary is probably the easiest approach to this essay. Take each monarch in turn and discuss how far his or her aims and opinions actually influenced religious policy. How necessary were they to the implementation of these policies? A balanced treatment also requires a discussion of the other factors which contributed to the religious changes. This is a good opportunity to refer to the visual imagery used to promote the supremacy.

**19**  How significant were the links between the English Reformation and the Reformation in Europe?

This essay must go beyond generalisation and include specific references to such links. Examples could include correspondence between English and continental theologians, influences on Cranmer's Prayer Books, the Marian exiles and their role in Elizabeth's reign. Descriptions of these links should lead to an assessment of their significance and there should be some element of balance that points to the differences between England and Europe and at times the conscious rejection of European ideas.

**20**  How justified is Christopher Haigh in talking of English Reformations rather than an English Reformation?

A student might make a good attempt at this essay on the basis of the title alone but a good start would be some acquaintance with Haigh's book *English Reformations* and particularly the introduction. The student could accept Haigh's views as they stand but would still need to provide his or her own argument for doing so; or reject his views, again giving reasons. Alternatively students might want to shift the emphasis, adopting some ideas and not others. Whatever the conclusion, there should be evidence of the student's own thoughts, not just a repetition of one historian's ideas.

## Specimen Essay Answer

How far can the Elizabethan religious settlement be regarded as the product of Elizabeth's own religious opinions?

At first sight it must seem that in 1559 Elizabeth had been successful in getting the religious settlement that best suited her beliefs. Requests for further reform were made throughout her reign, both by bishops and in Parliament, but she remained committed to the decisions of 1559. But as well as her personal preferences the settlement reflected a number of other influences: the demands of English Protestants, some returned from their exile in Mary I's reign, the resistance of the Catholic hierarchy and the need to take into account England's relations with other countries.

There can be no doubt that Elizabeth was a Protestant. Her refusal to allow the elevation of the host when mass was said in the royal chapel indicated her opinion of the Catholic doctrine of transubstantiation, and she made great play of her devotion to the English Bible in her procession through London on the eve of her coronation. A stop was brought to the heresy trials and a Twelfth Night entertainment at court was openly anti-papal. All this demonstrated her Protestant loyalties, but she also had conservative tendencies in religion. She insisted on retaining a crucifix and candlesticks in her own chapel, a cause for concern for many of her more ardent Protestant subjects. She insisted on the wearing of clerical vestments and she preferred, though she did not insist on, an unmarried clergy.

Elizabeth was helped in achieving this settlement by Sir William Cecil. He too was a Protestant and had already played a part in promoting Protestantism in the reign of Edward VI when he had chaired a conference on the Eucharist. He had links through marriage with a number of prominent Protestants. His father-in-law had been in exile during Mary's reign and his brother-in-law, Nicholas Bacon, had a long association with Matthew Parker who was to be Elizabeth's first Archbishop of Canterbury. Cecil himself had not gone into exile but his personal links helped when it came to getting the exiles' cooperation in Elizabeth's religious policy and his advice was often followed in the choice of bishops.

The Protestant exiles have in the past been seen as a major force in pushing through the settlement. J.E. Neale, in the 1950s, claimed that extreme Protestants, dominated by returned exiles, were so strong in the House of Commons that they forced through a settlement that was more extreme than Elizabeth had intended. This view has since been challenged. There were some returned exiles in the Commons and there were also some on Elizabeth's Council, who had also served Edward VI. However, they do not appear to have been extreme in their demands and they were still to a great extent loyal to the second Prayer Book of Edward VI's reign which was to be the basis of Elizabeth's settlement. Returned exiles like Cooke, Cecil's father-in-law, were to help put through Elizabeth's uniformity bill.

Many of the exiles were later to become bishops or high officials in the Elizabethan Church and to play an important role in implementing the settlement. As such they did tend to follow a 'hard line' and to feel that the 1559 settlement was a starting-point for reform rather than its conclusion.

Early in the reign, for example, they clashed with the Queen when she ordered the restoration of roods to the parish churches. Faced with the possibility of her new bishops resigning, Elizabeth had to give in on this issue and images were removed from churches throughout the country.

However, the main problem faced by Elizabeth in getting her settlement through Parliament was presented by the Catholic hierarchy. N.L. Jones has restored the Catholic bishops to their role of most effective opposition, a role in which their contemporaries certainly saw them. In February a bill making the Queen Supreme Head and allowing the imposition of a Protestant Prayer Book was effectively blocked by the united opposition of the bishops and a number of lay peers in the Lords. They amended the bill, removing any mention of the Prayer Book and refusing to authorise the supremacy title. This was not good enough for Elizabeth and the bill was dropped. After this failure a debate was arranged between Catholic and Protestant spokesmen with the probable aim of discrediting the Catholics and so reducing the effectiveness of their opposition. The actual debate may have had little impact but it resulted in the imprisonment of two Catholic bishops and so two less 'opposition' votes in the Lords. This tactic proved its worth in the following session when the bishops failed narrowly in preventing the passage of the Uniformity and Supremacy bills.

Although Catholic opposition failed to stop the settlement, it did win some concessions. In the debate on the supremacy bill the bishops successfully inserted a definition of heresy which meant that Catholics could not be accused of being heretics. Elizabeth also ordered the removal of offensive references to the Pope in the Prayer Book and the addition to the Prayer Book of the words on the Eucharist that had been used in the first Prayer Book of 1549. This wording allowed a wide interpretation of the book's position on the real presence. The adoption of the title Supreme Governor rather than Supreme Head can also be interpreted as a sop to the conservatives, although it was also commended by Protestants.

The international situation also played a part in the process of the settlement. Elizabeth could not at first be too radical in religion since on her accession England was still at war with France and needed to maintain good relations with Catholic Spain. The final settlement did not come about until peace had been signed with France. The Lutheran states in Germany were seen as potential allies for England and ambassadors to those states were given instructions to say that Elizabeth accepted the Augsburg Confession, that is that she was effectively a Lutheran. When the Thirty-Nine Articles were produced in 1563, Elizabeth ordered the removal of Article Twenty-Nine since it would be offensive to Lutherans. While never denying her own Protestantism, Elizabeth was always willing to allow others to draw their own conclusions on her beliefs if ambiguity served her purpose.

The settlement of 1559 certainly seemed to conform to most of Elizabeth's ideas on religion. She made some concessions to win over her more conservative subjects, although these do not appear to have been against any of her personal convictions, and the actual passage of the settlement had to take into account the bishops in the House of Lords. As for her Protestant subjects, in 1559 most of them were only too glad to have some form of Protestant Church established and although they might express criticism later in the reign they proved cooperative in bringing about the initial settlement. Elizabeth set out to achieve the royal supremacy and the use of the 1552 Prayer Book and these were the basis of the settlement that she refused to change for the rest of her reign.

# BIBLIOGRAPHY

The following is a very selective list of books from the large number available on the English Reformation. They are well written and well worth reading, and where they take a particular bias towards the subject this is clear to the reader.

**John Lotherington, ed:** *The Tudor Years* (Hodder and Stoughton, 1994). This is a good basic textbook of the period as a whole. The sections on religion are easy to find and will provide most of the information needed as a background to the documents in this book.

**A.G. Dickens:** *The English Reformation,* 2nd edition (Batsford, 1989). One of those books that is often described as a 'classic account' and it deserves it. This is a very full treatment of the Reformation, especially strong on the Protestant point of view, and this second edition takes into account, but does not always give way to, some more recent studies. Every student should read at least some of this book.

**J.J. Scarisbrick:** *The Reformation and the English People* (Blackwell, 1984). An early example of 'revisionism' at work. This is not a difficult book to read and deals clearly with the resistance to religious change and the methods used to overcome this resistance.

**E. Duffy:** *The Stripping of the Altars* (Yale, 1992). This is a large book and most students will ignore the first part on late medieval religion – a detailed and, if you have time, fascinating account. The account of the Reformation itself concentrates on resistance and gives a wide range of examples. The emphasis is on the positive aspects of traditional religion.

**Christopher Haigh, ed:** *The English Reformation Revised* (Cambridge, 1987). This is an excellent collection of essays on a number of Reformation topics. They include a survey of previous writing on the subject.

**Christopher Haigh:** *English Reformations* (Oxford, 1993). A survey of the religious changes under the Tudors which seeks not only to examine their impact but also to account for them.

**Christopher Harper-Bill:** *The Pre-Reformation Church in England* (Longman Seminar Studies, 1989). A relatively short and well-organised survey of the late medieval church. The aim of the book is to show that the Church was healthy and flourishing. There is a short collection of documents at the end.

**Robert Tittler:** *The Reign of Mary I* (Longman Seminar Studies, 1983). This is a general account of the reign but it contains a useful section on her religious policy. On the whole he takes a very favourable view of Mary. There is a short collection of documents at the end.

**Susan Doran:** *Elizabeth I and Religion* (Routledge, Lancaster Pamphlets, 1994). This is a very good and up-to-date survey of the religious policies and changes of Elizabeth's reign. This is well worth using by A-level students.

**Keith Randell:** *Henry VIII and the Reformation in England* (Hodder and Stoughton, Access to History Series, 1993).

**Nigel Heard:** *Edward VI and Mary: A Mid-Tudor Crisis?* (Hodder and Stoughton, Access to History Series, 1993)

**John Warren:** *Elizabeth I: Religion and Foreign Affairs* (Hodder and Stoughton, Acccess to History Series, 1993).

These three books are aimed at A-level students. They provide a clear survey of the topic with references to modern historians and contemporary sources

# INDEX